SUCCESS IN NEW HOME SALES

Developing The Right Mentality and Techniques

---

by Richard Tiller

Copyright ©1991 by Richard Tiller. All rights reserved. No part of this publication may be reproduced, stored in a retrieval system, or transmitted in any form or by any means without permission from the author.

Printed in the U.S.A. by Tiller Marketing Services
P.O. Box 531
Herndon, Va. 22070-0531.
ISBN: 0-9630-722-0-X
Library of Congress Catalog Card Number 91-91190

Contents

	Introduction	**5**
Chapter 1	Who Succeeds in New Home Sales?	**7**
Chapter 2	The First Ten Minutes	**23**
Chapter 3	Overcoming Objections	**47**
Chapter 4	Creating Value	**65**
Chapter 5	Demonstrating Your Product	**77**
Chapter 6	Showing Lots	**87**
Chapter 7	Closing	**103**
Chapter 8	Follow Up	**115**
Chapter 9	Difficult Situations	**121**
Chapter 10	Slumps and Burnout	**137**
Chapter 11	Review	**143**

Introduction

The purpose of this book is to help you achieve success in new home sales by developing a **Successful Sales Mentality**. A solid mental foundation allows effective techniques to develop naturally. A successful mentality for new home sales combines thorough preparation with an understanding of customers' needs, market challenges and specific on-site problems. It develops strategies for meeting these challenges and keeping the selling process focused toward the close. Ultimately it makes your performance more effective, and your career more successful and fulfilling.

Selling new homes is an art. It requires imagination, inspiration and the ability to ignite positive emotions. It is also a craft requiring discipline, knowledge, patience, energy and skill.

The primary "force" in new home sales is momentum. This book will explore momentum in detail: what it is, where it comes from, how to get it started, and how to avoid losing it.

The primary "skill" in new home sales is, believe it or not, preparation — a critical element in the new home sales mentality. The right mentality with the right preparation gives your selling tremendous vitality. It also makes your other selling skills more powerful, easier to learn, and much more natural to use.

I will discuss technique in great detail. It will be discussed in the context of a **Successful Sales Mentality** in which the technique becomes natural. Memorization will be minimal.

You will be able to develop benevolent aggressiveness, the strongest and most persuasive force in new home sales.

I will discuss the secrets of success of other top salespeople, and how they sustain that success over the long haul.

As you analyze the many potential pitfalls in new home sales, you will learn how the same mentality which generates momentum can also help you develop strategies to avoid these pitfalls.

In short, the goal of this book is to make success in new home sales come naturally.

CHAPTER ONE

Who Succeeds in New Home Sales?

Why choose a career in New Home Sales?

Many people don't start out pursuing a career in new home sales. It just happens to them. And then it grows on them. That is the way it happened with me.

I had never met a new home salesperson when I applied for my first sales job in 1972. I had not even been aware that the career existed. I was twenty-two years old, with a B.A. in cultural anthropology, and was frustrated because I could not find a job in my field. I needed something to tide me over until a "real job" came along, and a friend whom I respected suggested that I try selling new homes.

It turned out to be an enormously gratifying career for me, as it has been for many thousands of others. New home sales, if approached with an attitude of caring, diligence, responsibility, honesty and commitment, offers an enormously significant service to a large number of people. You are helping people improve their lives, and you are paid well to do it.

It's not for everybody. But for those who are suited to it, the career offers all the rewards which might be expected, and many more which are pleasant surprises.

What kind of a person is "suited" to a career in new home sales? I have always been fascinated by this question, and have had the opportunity to pursue it by serving on local and national sales award judging panels, and by studying techniques of top salespeople whom I have had the honor of knowing. Stereotypes are dangerous, so I will not attempt to define a "typical" new home salesperson. But I have found that many top salespeople share certain characteristics which give them an advantage over their competition.

Characteristics of Successful New Homes Salespeople

One of the great things about new home sales is that so many different kinds of people can succeed — Type A personalities and Type B, shy people and gregarious people, people oriented toward intellectual, spiritual, or social pursuits, methodical disciplinarians and free-spirited mavericks. But even from this rich variety of personalities, generalizations can be made about what makes them successful. Patterns emerge in their approach, or mentality, which allow their success or failure to be predictable. (By "success" I mean long-term success — the ability of the salesperson to maximize his or her productivity year after year under a variety of conditions.)

For the rest of this chapter I will briefly discuss the characteristics of successful salespeople. In future chapters I will bring these characteristics to life in the selling environment. Most of the elements of a successful sales mentality are available to everyone. But the more natural and obvious they seem to you, the easier it will probably be for you to master the art and craft of new home sales.

▪ *Personal Warmth*

Personal warmth is critical in establishing rapport with your buyer. It is a much different characteristic from the "gift of gab" so often associated with sales success. It cannot be faked. It comes from the heart, not the mouth, and helps you to break down the customer's resistance to your credibility and your probing questions. Customers must sense caring, not greed. They will only relate to you if they want to, and they will only want to if they do not feel threatened. A non-threatening demeanor is an extension of personal warmth.

■ *A Non-threatening Demeanor*

To sell a new home, you must **raise your prospect's comfort level to the point where the sale becomes inevitable.** This mindset is more important in new home sales than in other types of sales. Successful new home sales is not defeating your prospect in a battle of wills. The prospect's comfort level is a critical factor. Buying a new home is a traumatic experience — a decision which will have a major long-term impact on the buyer's lifestyle and financial condition. The less threatened and more cared-for your customers feel from the beginning, the more likely they are to buy in the end.

No matter how aggressive customers may act, they are generally frightened. One of the earliest goals in your interaction with the customer is to eliminate threatening stimuli from the selling environment. Unfortunately, one of the most threatening stimuli is frequently the salesperson himself. While a non-threatening demeanor grows partly out of your personal warmth, it is also related to many of the other characteristics which follow.

■ *Compassion*

Top salespeople genuinely care for their customers. They realize that it is not enough to merely tolerate or humor the customer. They know that true caring cannot be faked. Customers have a keen sense for a salesperson's level of compassion. When they sense that the salesperson's concern for their well-being is genuine, they will frequently add real value to the product in their minds. That is a fact which top salespeople have seen proven time after time. A caring salesperson will frequently make a sale that a more selfish salesperson could not make because the customer's level of confidence more quickly reaches the point where he or she is willing to buy.

A compassionate salesperson is able to proceed more naturally through the qualifying process because the prospect feels less threatened.

Compassion and personal warmth are characteristics which appear more frequently among the "survivors" in new home sales — those salespeople who weather the tough storms. Salespeople who lack these two characteristics tend to burn out faster, because they do not have as deep a sense of purpose in what they do. The more superficial approach to selling does not have the staying power in a profession as emotionally volatile as this.

"Caring," however, is not the same as "getting personally involved," or "taking the buyer's side." A salesperson must maintain objectivity, and must respect his fiduciary responsibility to the seller. Caring is more empathy than sympathy. It is genuine concern for identifying, relating to and fulfilling the prospect's needs. Fulfilling needs is the kingpin in successful new home selling. Identifying and fulfilling buyers' needs is a vital part of the mentality for success in selling, and is a critical skill for the salesperson to develop.

■ *Patience*

Patience is important not only in dealing with customers, but in dealing with your own environment or situation. "Survivors" in our business have a long-term mentality. They have the "short-term" patience necessary to deal with customers, recognizing their unique needs and anxieties. They also realize that long-term patience is just as important, especially on a bad project, in a personal slump, or in a market downturn. Top salespeople develop the ability to see beyond their current situation and to put that situation into a well-balanced perspective within a long-term scheme. They are able to accept slumps as inevitable and persevere through them. And they see market slowdowns as an opportunity to revitalize and sharpen their selling skills, which accumulate rust in easy markets even in the best of the superstars.

Patience is also a part of giving good service. As our products become more expensive and our industry more competitive, homebuilding is becoming a more service-oriented business. This fact leads into the importance of our next characteristic.

■ Ability to Sell Both Product and Service

Selling is frequently divided into two types: product selling and service selling. New home sales is one of the few sales professions which emphasizes both dimensions equally. Top salespeople in our field do not focus exclusively on product selling or service selling. Their mentality is balanced, realizing that with an investment as large as a home, buyers need assurance in both areas.

I have been impressed over the years with the fact that an overwhelming majority of top salespeople in our industry, unlike most other industries, actually do not consider money their top priority. While money is certainly a legitimate motivation, the long-term superstars believe that if they do their job right, the money will take care of itself. Top salespeople are very service-oriented, toward both their buyers and their company. A service-oriented mentality allows skills in identifying and fulfilling needs to develop much more naturally. It also makes product selling more credible and effective.

■ Honesty

Credibility is critical to success in new home sales. In a profession where your customers become your neighbors, dishonesty is dangerous. More importantly, the mentality for success which has been discussed up to this point could not exist without honesty at its foundation. The customer's trust of the salesperson allows that customer to overcome his fears and put his fate into the hands of someone about whom he knows relatively little. Honesty also becomes the basis of the next characteristic of success.

■ A Genuine Sense of Fairness

While your primary loyalty must always be to your seller (in most cases the builder), top salespeople are able to deal constructively with dilemmas between buyer and seller. They are able to remove self-interest from the equation to the point where they can defend their company's position with conviction as long as that position is fair and ethical. This level of integrity and strength also gives them credibility with their builder on those occasions when they genuinely believe the builder is making a mistake. When the builder can respect both the loyalty and the fair-mindedness of the salesperson, it is much easier for the builder to take the salesperson's advice in problem-solving strategies. Establishing this level of credibility often takes patience on the part of the salesperson. Having this kind of reputation is well worth the time and effort it takes to develop.

Customers normally respond to the quality of fair-mindedness in a salesperson with respect. While the customer's responses may not always be docile, they feel safer surrendering some of the control of the selling environment to this type of salesperson.

■ Confidence

A caring yet confident demeanor is very appealing. A customer will warm up to this type of personality much more quickly and easily than to an aloof or timid personality.

Selling requires a lot of courage, because there is a lot of adversity. This adversity should be faced head-on. Articulating a product's advantages is the easy part of selling. Facing your product's shortcomings must be done in a way which demonstrates your pride in the product, but also shows that you truly care for the well-being of your customer. You will not make every sale, because your product is not for everybody. Don't run scared, but don't show arrogance. Maintain your objective of fulfilling the needs of your prospect. A willingness to face objections and shortcomings head-on, and in a manner which places the buyer's well-being at the top of the priority list will gain more sales than it loses. It will also leave those who do buy from you better satisfied and more likely to refer future sales. This mentality grows naturally out of the characteristics of success already discussed.

How does ego fit into the whole idea of confidence?

While conceit does not work in the long run in new home sales, neither will ambivalence. In this type of selling, confidence requires a strong but controlled ego. Sometimes the word "ego" seems to take on a negative connotation. The type of ego I'm talking about here is nothing to feel awkward about. A strong ego is one legitimate testimony to our true value and to our strength of purpose.

Top new home salespeople maintain a healthy balance of ego and empathy. The importance of your own value and what you stand for must be balanced with the value of your buyers and their personal needs. This balance forms the basis of your confidence, and is much of what determines how appealing you are personally to your customers.

Confidence also provides the fuel for aggressiveness. Aggressiveness is vital to success in selling. The word "aggressive," like the word "ego," has taken on negative connotations in selling. It has become associated with hard sell. Our success in new home sales will depend largely upon our ability to draw a line between aggressiveness and hard selling. Hard sell rarely works in home sales any more. Hard sell means trying to win a battle of wills against your buyer, and is difficult to execute without becoming obnoxious. It usually fails because it is too threatening. Aggressive selling does not have to be threatening or obnoxious. *You are simply continuing the transaction until the buyer stops you. Aggressiveness is not about conquering; it is about developing and sustaining momentum.* There is nothing abusive or unkind about this type of aggressiveness. I like to call it *benevolent aggressiveness:* moving toward the resolution of an issue which both you and your customer want resolved.

Confidence is critical to a salesperson's ability to generate momentum in the selling process. A salesperson who lacks confidence is, ironically, more likely to stop the sales transaction than the prospect is. The confident, aggressive salesperson knows that only the prospect should interrupt the selling process, and pursues his or her strategy accordingly.

■ *Goal-Oriented*

Top salespeople develop the ability to envision and articulate their short-term and long-term goals, and then to stay focused on these goals until they achieve them.

Once you establish a goal, it is important to create a *clear image* of the *achieved goal* in your mind. Envision the accomplishment, and envision your life once the accomplishment has been completed. This vision will help sustain your enthusiasm and sense of purpose many times along the road to that accomplishment, especially during discouraging times.

After you have envisioned the goal, create another vision of the *path to the goal*. Envisioning the path will help you to stay focused. Sometimes you must choose between several paths, and you are not always certain which is the correct one. You may even have to switch paths along the way. Envision several paths at the beginning if you need to, but focus most clearly on your first choice. Keep the alternative paths in your peripheral vision, and bring them into focus if the need arises. Always make sure that your vision of the *achieved goal* and the *primary path* remain clearly focused throughout your journey.

Once your goal and path have been envisioned, *write them down* in as much detail as possible. Putting this information in writing makes it more permanent, tangible, organized, manageable and, of course, easier to remember.

The confidence discussed above gives energy to the characteristic of being goal-oriented. The next characteristic — perseverance—is equally vital to achieving your goals.

■ *Perseverance*

Perseverance adds an active dimension to the quality of patience. Perseverance is more than just hard work. It is more than merely toughing out a situation. Perseverance is a relentless desire to beat the odds — a long-term tenacity which enables you to hang in there until you win, and until your personal potential is maximized. It requires a positive attitude in the face of adversity.

Salespeople with this type of perseverance are able to tough out the hard times, in part, by remembering their previous successes. They realize that their past strengths are still there, even when the results are temporarily discouraging.

They frequently have a vision for greatness which transcends their day-to-day circumstances. This vision is part of a mentality which stays focused on the higher aspects of their profession, and on the pursuit of excellence in fulfilling their calling. Their ability to envision success keeps them from getting lost on the inevitable detours.

Driving from New York to San Francisco is a wonderful experience. But along the way you are bound to encounter traffic jams, road construction, countless gas station stops, and maybe even flat tires or mechanical failures. Perseverance involves keeping a clear vision of the Golden Gate Bridge, the Pacific Ocean, and many of the beautiful and exciting experiences along the way. If the trip turns out to be harder than you anticipated, then the destination will be all the better when you arrive. This is the mentality behind most of the long-term success stories in new home sales.

I have been amazed at the extent to which the top salespeople are idealists. Their values, their visions, the satisfactions which fulfill them are frequently on a higher plane than those of their peers. Being visionaries, their visions and values are the energy behind their perseverance.

But top salespeople are by no means just wishers and dreamers. While they sometimes communicate better with spoken words than through paperwork, there are a number of practical skills which salespeople must perfect in order to maximize their effectiveness. One of these skills is, in fact, paperwork.

■ *Paperwork*

This part of the new home sales job is considered by many salespeople to be the most tedious, and therefore the least worthy of their attention. A salesperson with a long-term winner's mentality appreciates the importance of paperwork as one of the fuels which keeps the builder's engine running. It is critical to the well-being of the customer, and the marketing research aspect of paperwork will repay you handsomely in terms of more effective sales and marketing strategies.

■ Understanding Your Company's Systems

Another of the seemingly more mundane parts of the job is understanding how your builder's systems integrate. These systems include marketing, purchasing, accounting, production and customer service. As with paperwork, sales superstars tend to have more of a "big-picture" mentality. They see the potential profit in understanding all of the builder's systems — even accounting. Understanding the total operation will not only make the sales part of the operation run more smoothly by being consistent with the other systems, but it will enable you to communicate more effectively the soundness and expertise of your company to your customers. While knowledge of this type may seem tedious, it is the type of knowledge which goes a long way in increasing your prospect's comfort level, and provides you with a significant selling advantage over less articulate competitors.

Knowledge of your company's systems will also help you to create more effective solutions to sales problems which might arise at your project, and solutions which will be more easily accepted by managers in other departments.

These principles apply to the next three characteristics of a successful selling mentality as well.

■ Knowledge of Construction

This asset will be discussed in greater detail in the sections on demonstrating models and showing lots. Product knowledge is one of the most powerful competitive tools for the sales superstars, distinguishing them as more credible, more sophisticated and more caring than their competition. Knowledge of construction goes far toward increasing the buyer's comfort level, and ultimately toward giving you more control over your selling environment.

■ Knowledge of Financing

As with knowledge of construction, knowledge of financing will enable you to function more as a "counselor," and less as a "salesperson." It will give you, your product and your builder more credibility and more value in the eyes of your prospective buyer.

■ *Knowledge of Your Market and Your Competition*

Top salespeople know their competition and use this knowledge to build credibility and value.

Sooner or later, in one way or another, the element of competition enters into nearly every real estate sale. Rarely do buyers see only one product during their search for a new home. The moment of truth arrives not when they decide to buy a new home, but rather when they decide which home to buy.

While "knocking" your competition is more likely to hurt your credibility than to help it, it is still essential for you to show your prospects why your home is the best for them of all the available alternatives, and better for them than where they are living now. Comparing yourself in specific detail to models at competitive communities is frequently one of the critical steps toward closing a sale.

Top salespeople become experts in marketing as well as sales. The last several characteristics of success which I have discussed could all be lumped under the heading of "expertise," and most consumers attach additional value to a product which is sold by an expert. Think of the retail business. A low level of expertise is typically associated with discount retailers, while a high level of professionalism justifies the retailer charging full price. In our business, those who are most successful over the long haul are not merely salespeople, they are housing industry experts. While developing this expertise takes extra time and effort, the sacrifice is viewed by the superstars as an investment with a very high rate of return.

Knowledge of your market and competition also helps you to track your own progress and provide better feedback to your builder.

■ *Intelligence*

There is no denying that being "fast on your feet" is an asset in new home sales. Thinking quickly helps you to sustain momentum, overcome objections, provide timely and relevant anecdotes which help to increase the buyer's comfort level, and come up with quick solutions to stumbling blocks.

There are several types of intelligence which are helpful in new home sales. (I emphasize the word "helpful." While intelligence is clearly an advantage, there are other assets which are far more valuable.)

"Wittiness" can be an appealing form of intelligence, and can often lighten the atmosphere of the selling environment. This can sometimes help the momentum to flow more easily.

"Quick-wittedness," a cousin of wittiness, enables the salesperson to bounce back from a negative response, and can also be helpful in keeping the buyer's attention.

The value of various types of "knowledge" has already been discussed.

"Empathy" and "sensitivity" must certainly be considered forms of intelligence in this type of selling. These two assets are particularly important in helping prospects to deal with their fears, overcome their objections and resolve their dilemmas as they progress toward the decision-making stage.

The "ability to reason" is a dimension of intelligence which adds power to selling your concept, keeping your buyer focused, overcoming objections and closing.

While certain types of intelligence are sometimes considered gifts, "preparation" is the discipline which enables intelligence to flourish. Preparation facilitates intelligence, and is therefore a form of intelligence in itself.

■ *A Sense of Humor*

A sense of humor is vital to long-term success. It is part of a healthy perspective which allows you to have a long-term, big-picture mentality toward a career which is filled with up-and-down-cycles and short-term frustrations. Up to this point I have been discussing the more serious, diligent and responsible elements of success. Top salespeople combine these more serious virtues with a sense of humor which frees them emotionally from the many types of temporary turmoil which they encounter. Salespeople who succeed in balancing this combination of seriousness and humor are the ones who sell the most — and last the longest.

■ *A High Level of Energy*

Stamina, both emotional and physical, is a treasure which needs to be carefully protected. Sales takes energy. Energy may take a different form in a good market than it takes in a bad market. It may have a different meaning in March than it has in August. But physical health and emotional freshness must not be underestimated. While the strongest will in the world can certainly be energizing, the ability to pace yourself in our seasonal, cyclical business is equally important.

Keeping a sense of personal balance in your life affects your energy level. So does an understanding and acceptance of the ebbs and flows of the market's rhythms. Storing up energy for the busy times and pressing on when you're exhausted is part of that rhythm. Using the slower times to redirect your energy into channels which enable you to add to your knowledge and experience, or simply to recharge your batteries, is just as important.

■ *Self-sacrifice*

Several years ago a study was done to determine what single characteristic was most frequently present in people who succeeded, and most frequently absent in people who failed. The study covered a variety of different types of jobs. Attributes such as diligence, commitment, intelligence, creativeness and knowledge were naturally found more often in successful people than in failures, although many people failed with one or more of these admirable traits. When the study was completed, the one characteristic which most clearly distinguished the long-term successes from the failures was ***a willingness to do things which other people were unwilling to do.***

Long-term superstars in new home sales are remarkably service-oriented. They also tend to be more humble than the less successful ones. Years ago when I began forming my list of the top characteristics of successful salespeople nationwide, I would not have expected this characteristic to top the list. But it has been as true in our profession as it has been in most others. As I have gained a better understanding of the other characteristics of success, I now realize it is this characteristic which lies at the heart of the successful new home sales mentality. A mentality of self-sacrifice provides a sort of greenhouse in which the other characteristics of success can grow and blossom.

It makes a good conclusion to the list.

SUMMARY

There are many effective skills and techniques for selling new homes. They are developed through training, experience and trial and error.

The foundation for these skills and techniques is a mentality which ties together many characteristics of the most successful salespeople. For a salesperson with a mentality for success, effective skills and techniques develop quickly and easily.

In this chapter we discussed nineteen elements of a **Successful Sales Mentality** which help to characterize many of the superstars of our profession.

1. Personal warmth
2. A non-threatening demeanor
3. Compassion
4. Patience
5. Ability to sell both product and service
6. Honesty
7. A genuine sense of fairness
8. Confidence
9. Goal-oriented
10. Perseverance
11. Paperwork
12. Understanding your company's systems
13. Knowledge of construction
14. Knowledge of finance
15. Knowledge of your market and your competition
16. Intelligence

17. A sense of humor
18. A high level of energy
19. Self-sacrifice

With this mental foundation now in place, we can construct the framework for a successful selling strategy, which begins with establishing rapport and generating momentum. We will then focus on refining the skills and techniques which accelerate the momentum toward the final close.

The value of *preparation* as a primary selling skill will be emphasized throughout this book. Preparation helps you to sell from a position of strength. The end of the first eight chapters will feature one or more "action items" which will help you to apply the main principles in that chapter to your preparation.

Action Items

1. It is important to be aware of your own "characteristics of success." This awareness will not only increase your confidence, it will also make your execution more effective. Review the list shown above in the Summary, and add any additional characteristics which you believe make you exceptional. It is important that you write this list down for three reasons:
   a) It will help you to focus on your strengths so that you can take maximum advantage of them in your selling strategy.
   b) You will want to refer back to this list if you slip into a slump and need to restore your confidence and focus.
   c) You will be able to add to the list as you develop new strengths.
2. Make a list of those characteristics about yourself which you believe you must strengthen in order to become more successful. Then work out a plan for personal growth in those areas.

CHAPTER TWO

The First Ten Minutes

"The first ten minutes" (your first face-to-face interaction with the prospect) is perhaps the most underestimated step in the selling process. A friendly greeting, a brochure, a brief overview of the builder, the community and the product, and then directing the prospect to the models: these steps are frequently "all that should be expected" in your initial meeting with the prospect. Yet these steps are not enough for one primary reason: they fail to generate momentum, and momentum in new home sales is everything. The first ten minutes is, in fact, the point in the selling process at which the actual momentum of the sale should begin.

It may seem impossible to generate momentum in a transaction before the prospect has seen the models, but the truth is that momentum should begin before the prospect sees the first model. If momentum can be achieved before the models are seen, then the prospect can evaluate the models in a more favorable frame of mind.

It is very important to have control of the selling environment. That control begins in the first ten minutes, and your words and actions during that time should set the tone for the entire transaction.

Successfully controlling the selling environment requires the proper mentality as you develop your transaction. As you develop an approach which will help you to generate momentum, you also look into the mind of the customer. Keeping your mentality in sync with that of your buyer will help you to establish rapport, create momentum, and ultimately gain control of the selling environment.

Now let's meet "SAM." SAM is the new home salesperson's best friend, and will be our companion throughout the rest of this book. SAM is our **Strategy to Achieve Momentum** — a vital part of a **Successful Sales Mentality**.

The Strategy To Achieve Momentum

The primary key to success in new home sales is to structure the entire sales transaction, from initial greeting to closing, around a **Strategy to Achieve Momentum** (SAM). Each of these three crucial words has its own particular significance.

Strategy — This word means you have a plan. Planning is critical in new home sales. One of the best uses you can make of your "down time" — your time in between customers and phone calls — is preparation. The planning process includes gathering knowledge of your competition and your own product (including particular units for sale), and preparation for dealing with specific objections. You need to conceptualize and plot out the direction of your selling presentation before you meet your first prospect. Naturally, your presentation will vary with each customer as you learn more about their individual personalities and needs, but you still need a path to follow, a preconceived sequence of events designed to help you achieve and sustain momentum.

Achieve — Momentum does not just happen. It is the result of a series of actions directed toward one specific goal — developing and sustaining momentum. Since it is rarely the customer who will take responsibility for momentum in the selling process, momentum is truly an "achievement" by the salesperson, and an enormously significant one.

Momentum — Momentum is the force which keeps the selling process moving ahead. Keeping momentum alive is one of the most challenging, and often most frustrating, parts of new home sales. The goal of SAM is to provide a strategy which puts the primary emphasis on momentum. SAM consists of a sequence of selling stages which revolve around the whole concept of momentum. ***Momentum is the single most important element in selling new homes,*** so the mentality and the strategy which you develop to sell your homes should focus on momentum more than anything else.

THERE ARE EIGHT STAGES TO SAM. Keeping the stages of your strategy in their proper sequence helps you to keep your strategy focused. Better still, each stage of SAM allows your momentum to continue, and as it continues, it is natural for the momentum to accelerate. Therefore, the farther you get in your strategy, the more likely you are to get to your next stage. This mentality keeps you focused on the objective of generating momentum, controlling your selling environment, and moving continuously toward the close.

Your goal in the first ten minutes is to begin to generate your momentum by accomplishing the first four stages of SAM. So the initial stages of closing do, in fact, begin when you first greet your prospect.

The eight stages of SAM are as follows:
1. Establish rapport with your customer.
2. Explain your concept to the customer.
3. Determine the customer's needs.
4. Show that your product fulfills the customer's needs.
5. Lead the customer to pick out a favorite model.
6. Lead the customer to pick out a favorite lot.
7. Create in the customer's mind the fear of losing that favorite lot.
8. Ask for the order.

Each of these stages in SAM relates naturally to the one which follows. If executed correctly, each stage can trigger the next, increasing the momentum much like a booster rocket. You must execute each stage with a clear vision of the next stage already in mind. This is why planning is so important. Remember, this strategy is not a series of "separate stages," but rather a series of evolving stages which are connected by the force of momentum.

Each stage grows into the stage which follows, and as the stages progress the momentum increases.

The first two stages of SAM will help you to start off by setting a different tone from that of your competitors. This is particularly important in highly competitive markets where prospects visit a large number of projects, and can quickly become tired, confused and frustrated.

Stage One — Establishing Rapport

Top salespeople develop relationships with their customers as quickly as possible in order to open up lines of communication.

Their interaction with the customer takes the form of a conversation, not a lecture. They build rapport throughout the relationship by searching for common ground and for areas of interest to the customer. Hopefully, the rapport will grow into trust as the relationship develops.

When you first greet your customer, start with whatever icebreaker makes you feel comfortable. You want to begin relating to your customers right away through some piece of mutually interesting piece of information: their car, the neighborhood, the local sports team, or some other form of non-threatening exchange which helps your customers relate to you as "another regular human being." But your customer still comes in expecting information, not a prolonged period of small talk. So it is not long before you are into your sales presentation. (The unusually friendly prospect with plenty of time on his hands is more the exception than the rule.)

Techniques for establishing rapport vary with the personality of the salesperson, and this is certainly an area where you should experiment and then stick with what works for you. While I do believe that you should begin your greeting with a handshake and an exchange of names, it is not necessary to withhold a brochure from the prospect for as long as possible. Establishing a non-threatening demeanor is paramount in establishing rapport.

There are a few innocent questions you need to ask early in

The First Ten Minutes

order to get a basic understanding of your prospect's situation. Questions like, "Are you familiar with our community?" or, "Do you live nearby?" will help you to orient your presentation and set the stage for getting further information about their needs and buying ability later in your presentation. However, you don't want to ask too many questions at the beginning. Remember, you are still a stranger to them, and they are probably not comfortable answering a string of questions from you at this point. You need to begin giving them the foundation of your presentation and establishing momentum as quickly as possible.

Most customers want to know your prices right up front. If you start out by trying to withhold information, your customers will be viewing your product with a chip on their shoulder. Why expose yourself to that risk when the chances of your gaining an advantage by withholding prices (or any other information which the customer requests) are minimal?

I also do not believe that customers must sign a guest card immediately. This can occasionally be another threatening stimulus. You should never ask for anything from the customers until you have given them something first. You should also not allow your customers to feel vulnerable at the beginning of your attempts to establish rapport with them. Allow yourself to become vulnerable first, and you will be perceived as being more human — like them — and less like a selling machine. Ask them to sign a guest card at the conclusion of your conversation in the sales office, or at the conclusion of your model tour.

Typically, the slower the market is, the harder it seems to establish rapport with your prospects. You will often find that the more sales offices your prospects have visited, the harder it is to establish rapport with them. There is too little individualism in sales presentations in the new homes business, especially in the first ten minutes. ***The more individualistic your presentation is, the better chance you have of holding the prospect's interest.***

As you see prospects approaching your sales office, imagine that they have been beaten up at the last five sales offices they visited. They are bruised and bloodied, and their defenses are up. They just want to get your prices and then be left alone to see your models. Your focus needs to be on providing an antidote to this mental state. Your demeanor should be designed to make them forget all that has gone before and focus on you, your builder, your community and your product. It needs to be a fresh experience for the customer. Consider their reluctance as an opportunity instead of an obstacle. You can use the blunders of your competition to your advantage, rather than being a victim of them. Your goal, after all, is to show your prospects that you are different, and better, than what they have seen up to this point, and what they will see from this point on.

In market downturns, buyers see impatience, irritation, frustration and failure in the actions of your competitors, and now they feel like victims. The antidote is kindness, friendliness, patience and concern. Your dignity, composure and confidence will imply that you, your builder and your product are the best there is. This approach will allow you to sell and establish rapport simultaneously.

Each stage of SAM grows into the next stage. Therefore, no stage ever stops: it becomes a part of each of the stages which follow. Establishing rapport does not end. It is the first stage of SAM because it is the stage upon which you must focus first in order to establish momentum. There is no need to overwork rapport at the very beginning. You can start stage two of SAM ("concept selling") within a minute or two of greeting your prospect, and then nurture the rapport and allow it to grow as you continue through your "first ten minutes."

Stage Two — Concept Selling

A good rule of thumb for gaining an early competitive advantage in your sales presentation is: ***Sell your concept first, and your product second.***

Instead of telling your prospect what your product is at the very beginning, start off by telling them "why" it is. ***The concept is a concise statement of your product's unique significance: why the product is important in the marketplace.*** It must be a statement which is easy for the prospect to grasp and remember. Why was the product designed in the first place? What is special about it? What puts it in a category apart from all the others? What makes it unique? Answering these questions defines your concept.

Set your product apart from your competition in as simplified and memorable a way as possible. Your goal is to carve out your own territory in the prospect's mind as quickly as possible, and then execute your presentation within that territory. You want to distinguish yourself from everybody else. Your competition all goes into one category. You go into the other category. This mentality is at the heart of "concept selling."

Articulate the concept on which your product is based — your product's reason for being — and then describe the features and benefits of the product within the context of the concept. The concept is the attention-getter, and is the foundation upon which the product pitch is based. Concept selling makes your product selling much more powerful, meaningful and memorable. That is why you sell the concept first and the product second.

The alternative is the more common approach: trying to move right into the product sale. By selling the product first, without putting it into the context of a concept, you throw yourself right into the middle of the competitive whirlwind of the marketplace before you have established an advantage. No matter how eloquent or well-prepared a product pitch may be, without a concept it still runs the risk of getting caught up in the barrage of competitors' product pitches. Sooner or later pure product pitches must inevitably degenerate into a price sell, a position from which only the lowest-priced product wants to make its stand. Unless you are the lowest-priced product in your marketplace (and, by the way, "lowest price" is a concept), you need to articulate a unique concept in order to stake out your own field upon which to wage your competitive battle. Establishing your concept is like having the homecourt advantage when you give your product presentation.

A concept differs from a "unique selling premise" in that it is broader in scope. A unique selling premise focuses primarily on what is "different" about your product from other products. *A concept explains not only your product's uniqueness, but also its importance.* It explains why the home is a "smarter value" — a more intelligent purchase and, where relevant, a wiser investment. The concept justifies the product's existence, and tells the prospect why they are better off buying yours than anyone else's.

Your concept may be your price. "We are the lowest-priced single family home in the area," or, "We are the lowest-priced single family home per square foot in the area," or "We are the lowest-priced single family home with a two-car garage (or with some other feature)." It may be that you have achieved the best sales rate in some specified period of time. Or it may be particular features: the home with the best family room in your price range, or the best master bedroom, or the best kitchen, or the best balance of several features.

Your concept may be that your builder set out to provide the best total value of any home under $200,000 by offering the best combination of location, lot size, and square footage. Or it may offer the "smartest" allocation of space — the largest percent of the home's total square footage placed in those parts of the home which statistically receive the most use. Or the most potential functions in those important areas.

You may want to position the benefits vs. sacrifices of your product as being more in tune with today's lifestyle priorities. Or you may be offering a "hybrid" product which offers the "best of both worlds:" a townhome or condo with the largest number of single family features, or a small lot single family home with smarter allocation of space and a smaller price tag.

Your concept may be something obvious or something subtle, something objective or something subjective. Your concept is whatever you say it is. Just be sure to say it early and say it clearly. Plant this seed in the prospect's mind first, before they hear about specific features and benefits, and before they see the models. They will then be learning about your product from your perspective, and not within the context of what the last salesperson told them. Don't force the prospect to figure out your concept for themselves. They probably won't.

Think of your concept as the territory you have staked out within the competitive marketplace. Naturally you have an advantage if your builder takes a concept orientation toward his site planning and product design.

As you gain experience and feedback at your project, the concept may evolve into something different than it started out to be, and that's OK. The important point is that your concept message should be credible, understandable and distinctive from the competition. If you are telling your prospects something informative and meaningful which they have never heard before, and which was conceived with the best interests of people like them in mind, they will be much more inclined to hear you out. They will be more willing to view your product within the context of what you have told them, and with a different mindset than the way they have viewed (or will view) the competition.

Stage Three — Determining Your Customer's Needs

As you establish rapport with a customer in the first ten minutes, you want to learn two things:
1. Why, of all the places that a customer could have chosen to go that day, did they choose your sales office?
2. What can you do to sell them a home?

Boiling these two questions down to their most basic form would leave you with this question:

"What do you need?"

This is the most important question in new home sales. It is more important than the question, "What do you want?" You should not necessarily be discouraged if you cannot give the buyer everything he wants. Neither can anyone else. To some extent, you even have the ability to influence what he wants. First you must find out what your customer needs, and then focus on the best way to meet those needs.

Need fulfillment is a basic element in any form of selling. Give the customer what they need at a price they can afford and they will buy. Selling would truly be that simple if only needs were that simple.

What are real needs? When does a desire become a need? How do you identify needs? How do you create needs? How do you point out needs which buyers have that they don't know they have?

As you already know, learning what your prospects' needs are, and determining how you may be equipped to fulfill those needs, begins with establishing rapport. You are your prospects' residential doctor. You must evaluate the symptoms of what is ailing them — that is, what it is they are lacking in their present living environment that they must have in their next one. You must formulate a diagnosis, and then provide a cure.

The first step in your treatment is to get the prospect to like you and trust you. This is why you start out by establishing rapport.

Some salespeople are uncomfortable asking probing, qualifying questions the minute a prospect walks in the door. If you are among these, as I am, you can start out with a brief exchange that is about something other than business. You can then proceed to a brief discussion about your concept, and conclude by asking where they live now, and what it is that is making them think about moving. This approach will help get you started on the road to determining the buyer's needs. As mentioned earlier, your interaction with the buyer should be a conversation. Not a lecture. And not an interrogation.

The subject of the buyer's needs is one which you can approach very directly. While certain qualifying questions, such as financial status, should be approached more discreetly, and after the prospect feels less threatened, questions involving their needs are both professional and appropriate. They should know up front that your focus is on providing for their needs, and not simply to sell them a home for the sake of the commission.

Examples of questions which help you to zero in on the prospect's needs early are:

"Where do you live now?"

"What is it that's made you think about moving?"

"How is your search coming? Are you seeing things that you like?"

"What's your number one priority for your next home?"

"What is the main thing you need in a home that you don't already have?"

For a preliminary qualifying question, you can tell them your price range and then simply ask them, "Is this the approximate price range you were trying to stay in?" While you should not go too far in trying to interpret their answer to this question, seeing and listening to their reaction is still more valuable than working in the dark, and is less threatening in the first ten minutes than asking their income and debt structure.

Need-identification questions should not replace the other types of qualifying questions ("Where do you work?" "How many are in your family?" etc.). On the contrary, most good qualifying questions are need-identification questions in one form or another. The point is to maintain a mentality throughout your qualifying process in which need fulfillment is the focus, as opposed to drifting into random interrogation. Some salespeople even explain to their customers point-blank that they are asking them about needs so that they can help determine more quickly whether particular homes may interest them. (This type of approach works for some, but is not comfortable for everyone.)

Determining your customers' needs and then helping them to fulfill those needs in terms of your product is selling in its highest, and most enlightened, form. It is the point at which selling becomes not only the craft which we discussed earlier, but a valuable service as well.

Why is determining the customer's needs at the outset so critical? One reason is that it helps you to make your presentation more individualistic. A second is that it helps you to set into motion your **Strategy to Achieve Momentum**.

A third reason is more subtle. Subconsciously, if not consciously, the buyer and seller are engaged in a battle for control of the selling environment. This is the primary source of psychological tension in the selling environment. The sooner the buyer believes that he is relinquishing control of the selling environment, the more threatened he feels. As the relationship between the buyer and the seller develops, if the seller succeeds in establishing rapport, credibility and trust with the buyer, the buyer may ultimately be willing to surrender control of the selling environment to the seller. But at the beginning the buyer wants control. "Give me the prices, let me see the models, and leave me alone. If I like what I see I will come back and ask questions. You will answer those questions and only those questions. Then I'll go home and think about it." That is typically the prospects' ideal scenario when they first walk into your sales office.

The primary benefit of developing the need-identification focus is that it allows you to build a bridge between your desire to control the selling environment and the prospect's desire to control it. As you begin fulfilling your prospect's needs, you also begin to gain control of the selling environment. This is because as long as you are fulfilling the prospect's needs, he believes he is controlling the selling environment, so he is happy.

What are some of the types of needs you should be attempting to determine? Although the list is endless, here are a few examples:

Price range

Location (Location is important to different people for different reasons, so be sure you know theirs: commuting to work, school district, proximity to church, conveniences, lifestyle, closeness to family, etc.)

Number of bedrooms

Security

A more exciting home

Needs relating to specific property uses

A particular feature or combination of features

Something about their current situation which is intolerable

Personal goals which may be part of their homebuying decision

Whenever possible, lead your prospects, through suggestion or questioning, to articulate needs which coincide with your product's greatest strengths.

Stage Four —
Show That The Product Fulfills The Customer's Needs

Not every person who walks into your sales office can have their needs fulfilled by your product. Nor would they necessarily be able to buy your product if it did fulfill their needs. Be as thorough as possible in probing and qualifying before determining that a prospect is not worth chasing. At least half of your prospects are worth chasing. After identifying their needs and qualifications you will realize that you can fulfill enough of their needs to give you as good a chance of selling to them as any of your competitors could have. They are worth competing for.

Naturally, very little of your goal of fulfilling buyers' needs is achieved in the first ten minutes, because the prospect has not yet seen your product, but setting the stage for this objective does occur in the first ten minutes. You want to learn enough about your prospect's needs and motivations to get them to view your models with a positive attitude — with a hope that this is perhaps just what they are looking for.

Here's an example of how this might work. The salesperson in this situation is working with a middle-income family who's outgrown their current home, but can't afford a huge payment increase. She is setting the stage for this family to view a moderately-priced single family home which has a small foyer, living room and childrens' bedrooms.

Salesperson: "What is it that's made you think about moving?"

Customer: "We're renting an older house now, and the rooms are just too small."

Salesperson: "Well, I hope we can solve that problem for you. Room sizes are one of the main reasons people buy our homes here. We've studied this problem a lot, and we've learned that a family like yours usually wants more space in the family room, the kitchen and the master bedroom. They also want the home to look good on the outside. At $100 a square foot, it's a shame to throw away your money on oversized foyers, living rooms and extra bedrooms when that's not really what you need. Our concept here is to spend your money where you spend your time."

The salesperson has learned just enough about the customers' basic needs to get them to focus favorably on her product, with both its strengths and weaknesses. She has positioned herself and her builder as knowledgable, caring and tuned into the needs of the market which they are trying to serve.

In the next example the salesperson is selling single-family homes on the smallest lots in her market, and the prospect is not very cooperative. So the salesperson's challenge is to generate a spark of interest in her customers before they see the models, and also to get the customers to focus more on what their needs really are.

Salesperson: "What is the main thing you need in a home that you don't already have?"

Prospect: "We don't know. We're just looking. When we see what we want, we'll know it."

Salesperson: "Well let me tell you a little about these, because they really are different. Most builders in this market put their homes on larger lots than we do, and that's fine because some folks want that. But each year more and more people are saying that they'd rather see their money go into the home, instead of into a larger lot that they have to maintain but will rarely use. Land has gone up in price faster than building materials, so unless you're going to use every square foot of the larger lot, you're better off getting a smaller lot and putting the extra money into things that you will use every day. Our concept here is that real value is more money in the home and less in the lot. Here you get a better kitchen, higher ceilings, a more comfortable master bedroom suite, and a more interesting looking home. All this in return for giving up fifteen feet of your back yard that you would rarely have used anyway, and the home takes less work to keep up. What do you think of that approach?"

Here the salesperson is accomplishing a number of things:
1. She is defusing her main objection right up front by positioning it as a benefit.
2. She is positioning her product as more individualistic.
3. She is positioning her product, and her builder, as more

intelligent. She is developing confidence in the builder as an innovator who bucks the system to provide a truly better home for his customer's money.
4. She is positioning her product as a better value.
5. She is not surrendering control of the selling environment to the prospect. She's turning the customer's desire for control into an opportunity to persevere, showing that she really cares about her customers and her product. As a result, instead of losing control she is establishing her own territory in the customer's mind.
6. She's selling her concept in order to establish the superiority of her product.
7. She's used market acceptance as proof that her concept is the right one. She's showing her customers that other people like them are glad they made the decision to buy into this more sophisticated concept, and their lives are better because of it. Third-party endorsements are a powerful tool in new home sales.
8. She concludes by attempting to elicit a response in order to have another opportunity to probe for information on the customer's needs.

In this example the salesperson had virtually nothing to work with in the way of information on the prospect's needs, so she had to take initiative and to generate momentum by telling how her product was designed to meet people's needs and how it has succeeded in achieving its goal. The hope is that if the salesperson perseveres in a caring yet confident way, the customers will eventually open up a little more, if they are legitimate prospects at all.

One more example. In this one the salesperson is selling townhomes at the high end of the market. Her prospects are a little more cooperative, but they had expected to buy a single family home for this amount of money.

Salesperson: "What's your number one priority for your next home?"

Prospect: "Well, to tell you the truth, we think we really want a single family home."

Salesperson: "How's your search coming? Are you seeing things you like?"

Prospect: "We've seen a couple of nice places."

Salesperson: "Is there anything in particular that kept you from buying them?"

Prospect: "I guess we just felt like they were overpriced. They were a lot of money and they just didn't have everything we wanted."

Salesperson: "Anything in particular?"

Prospect: "Oh, the master bedroom was too small in one. Or there wasn't enough cabinet space in the kitchen. At one place the house was nice but the neighborhood wasn't so hot."

Salesperson: "That's the problem with single family homes. To get one at a decent price you have to make so many compromises. A lot of people who bought here started out wanting a single family home, and then realized they could get more of what was really important to them in a townhome. I must admit, these homes cost as much as some of the single family homes in the area. But the homes are larger, the kitchens are better, and we can afford better quality for details like cabinets, trim, doors and windows. And people love the neighborhood. You really need to see these. They might give you exactly what you've been looking for."

Again the salesperson has defused her largest objection — price — while positioning her homes as fulfilling the customers' needs, even though the customers will have to alter their perspective in order to see the benefits. This is why approaching needs in the first ten minutes is so important. If the salesperson had not gone through that portion of SAM at the beginning, the customers would have walked into the models thinking, "This is just another townhome — what are we doing here anyway?"

The salesperson's message may have to be reinforced several more times before the customer is convinced, but at least they heard it once before they saw the models. Now they can view the models as a possible solution to their real needs, and not just from their prior perspective that townhomes are inferior to single family homes.

The secret to controlling the selling environment is to be constantly solving the buyer's problems. That is the one thing the buyer and seller both want. It is the primary common ground between the buyer and the seller during the sale. And establishing common ground is vital to establishing rapport. Solving buyers' problems is also the primary source of momentum in the selling process.

Focusing on the buyer's *real* and *specific* needs must be the thread which runs from the beginning of the selling encounter through the signing of the contract. As long as the focus of your sales approach is "providing service to the buyer" rather than trying to defeat him in a battle of wills, the buyer is not threatened and is willing to let his defenses down enough to allow you to effectively control the selling environment. As soon as you stop fulfilling needs (and are therefore demanding more than you are giving), the battle is on again and the buyer's defenses go back up.

As was stated earlier, you cannot usually expect to get too far with the goal of identifying and fulfilling needs in the first ten minutes, but you can at least lay the foundation and begin to carve out your own territory in the customer's mind.

Your ability to fulfill buyers' needs increases during your demonstration of the product, which is the subject of Chapter Five. A couple of points about product demonstration need to be made now in order to show how to begin building on the foundation which you have laid in the first ten minutes.

In the three examples just discussed, the salespeople were attempting to spark the beginning of the selling momentum. The next stage in the **Strategy to Achieve Momentum** will be to get the buyer to pick out a favorite model. You need to be thinking about how you will increase momentum during the model demonstration. (Remember, one of the keys to SAM is that in each stage you accelerate momentum by beginning to focus on the next stage.)

While keeping momentum going by providing problem-solving service during your model demonstration, you must also seek feedback continually to know whether you are unwittingly

pursuing a wrong track. Three examples of how to generate this feedback are as follows:
1. "When you said you were looking for a home that was more practical, is this family room/kitchen configuration the kind of improvement you had in mind?"
2. "We believe that a lot of builders underestimate the importance of the exterior of a home. We've tried to create the best-looking homes in our price range, and we think that is one of the reasons we've been so successful. What do you think?"
3. "Every one of our homes has convenient access from the garage to the kitchen. Our research has shown that this is very important to buyers, even though it's something that they often don't think of until after they've moved in. We always consider our potential customers to be our best source of information. Do you have anything that's particularly important to you that we either have or don't have?"

Some of the top salespeople feel perfectly comfortable asking their prospects as they go along whether they are in fact fulfilling the prospects' needs, and if not, why not. While their styles may vary in degree of directness, some approach the issue by telling the prospect at the outset that that's what they're trying to do, and that's what their builder is in business for. In effect, they tell their customers that they do their job best when they are fulfilling the customers' needs, and they ask the customer to keep them on track. While this is only one style, the point is to develop your own consistent style for getting feedback during model demonstration.

Whatever approach you choose for identifying and fulfilling your prospects' needs, the underlying principle is, ***If you listen carefully enough, your prospects will tell you how to sell them a home.***

Other Goals For The First Ten Minutes

In order to begin establishing momentum in the first ten minutes, your primary objectives are:

1. Developing rapport with your prospect;
2. Selling your concept;
3. Developing an understanding of your prospect's needs and motivations;
4. Making those needs and motivations the target of your selling focus. This approach is at the heart of a successful new home sales mentality.

There are also several other pieces of business which you must attend to during the first ten minutes in order to maximize your effectiveness:

1. ***Sell the location.***

Find out how much the prospect already knows about your location and tailor your presentation accordingly.

2. ***Sell the builder.***

Focus on those highlights of the builder's track record and philosophy which will help to increase the builder's credibility and the customer's comfort level.

3. ***Make your presentation enthusiastic.***

Good times or bad, customers really do buy primarily on emotion, and then justify their decision with reason. Enthusiasm is contagious, and so is lethargy. The more enthusiastic you are at the beginning, the easier it will be to get the customer emotionally involved once they have seen your product.

4. ***Start out as a counselor, not as a salesperson.***

You initial demeanor should be more that of an advisor than a seller. While you are beginning your **Strategy to Achieve Momentum** in the first ten minutes, you are also establishing rapport with as non-threatening a presence as possible. That is not to say that your demeanor is passive. It is, as stated earlier, "benevolently aggressive," not hard sell.

5. ***Do only the most basic financial qualifying.***

I believe that qualifying in the first ten minutes should normally not go too far beyond the following basic questions:

a. "Is there a particular time frame when you are planning to move?"
b. "Is this the price range you were planning to stay in?"
c. "Are you familiar with the income requirements for a home

in this price range?"

In general, personal financial qualifying occurs more comfortably after the prospect has shown an interest in a particular model which you are offering.

Summary

The first ten minutes should be more than just a greeting and an introduction to your product. These two objectives alone do nothing to help generate momentum, and therefore do little to help you sell. Your selling mentality, in order to be aggressive without being hard sell, must revolve around the salesperson's best friend, SAM **(Strategy to Achieve Momentum)**. SAM has eight crucial stages, each of which leads naturally to the next.
1. Establish rapport with your customers.
2. Explain your concept.
3. Determine your customer's needs.
4. Show that your product fulfills your customer's needs.
5. Lead the customer to pick out a favorite model.
6. Lead the customer to pick out a favorite lot.
7. Create in the customer's mind the fear of losing that favorite lot.
8. Ask for the order.

You get SAM into motion in the first ten minutes by working through the first four stages discussed in this chapter.

To establish rapport with your customer in the first ten minutes, you must establish an atmosphere which is warm, friendly, casual, and conversational (meaning that the interaction should be a conversation, not a lecture or an interrogation.) Your demeanor should be non-threatening, more like a counselor than a salesperson, and it should be confident, showing expertise as well as success.

An effective salesperson is "benevolently aggressive". Aggressiveness in new home sales means continuing through the steps of your planned strategy, one by one, until the customer causes the transaction to stop. An aggressive salesperson never stops the momentum himself.

Concept selling helps you to carve out your own territory in the competitive marketplace, and also your own territory in the buyer's mind. Part of developing a **Successful Sales Mentality** is developing a keen understanding of the buyer's mentality.

The better you can identify and fulfill your customers' needs, the more effectively you will be able to control the selling environment.

As you prepare your strategy for identifying needs, plan ways to get your customer to articulate needs which coincide with your concept and with the strengths of your product.

Explain how your product has succeeded in fulfilling the needs of others.

Point out needs which your customers may not even know they have.

Get feedback as you progress through the transaction so that you can stay on track in fulfilling your customers' needs.

You also want to use the first ten minutes to sell the location, sell the builder, convey enthusiasm, and touch on preliminary financial qualifying.

Focusing on SAM is critical to a successful new home sales mentality. If you can succeed in developing this mentality, then you don't have to worry about memorizing dozens of "tricks of the trade." Developing a **Successful Sales Mentality** will make your day-to-day selling efforts easier and more powerful for years to come.

Now that the first ten minutes are behind you, you are ready to enter into the more exciting and challenging stages of selling —the stages where momentum accelerates and begins to move toward the close. First I will examine that part of selling which most threatens momentum — dealing with customers' objections.

Action Items

1. Plan several strategies for establishing rapport quickly. Ideas may include:
    a. Icebreakers.

    b. Ways to establish common ground.
    c. Interesting pieces of information.

Note: Some salespeople write out scripts for themselves, as though they are acting on a stage. Their point is not to be "canned" or unspontaneous, but to develop a scenario which they can analyze objectively. The script is not intended to be repeated verbatim. It acts as a framework for your selling strategy, which you adapt to each customer individually. I found this tool very helpful in my own preparation. I wrote out scripts not only for the initial greeting, but for each of the stages in the selling sequence. If you have never tried this approach, you might want to experiment with it to see if it can add a dimension to the preparation of your strategy and presentation.

2. List the questions which you most need for the prospect to answer in the first ten minutes. Remember that your goal is to learn about the prospect's current situation, needs and motivations. You are a doctor attempting to make a diagnosis so that you can provide a cure. Your questions will have additional value if they can lead your discussion toward your product's strengths or concept.

3. Write out your concept so that you can convey it easily and with maximum impact early in the first ten minutes. Your concept should include:
    a. What you did.
    b. Why you did it.
    c. Whom you did it for.
    d. What your results have been (if this information is advantageous or provable).

4. List highlights about your location, builder and community which you want to emphasize before your prospect sees a model home.

5. List any third-party endorsements which may be relevant during the first ten minutes. While most third-party endorsements have greater impact during later stages of the sale, you may have one or two which are immediately relevant to your concept or your overall success story.

6. Set up a diary for significant thoughts and events of each

day. Information included in your diary may include:
a. Customer interactions and insights gained from these experiences.
b. Strategies considered.
c. Information gathered.
d. Significant communications with supervisors, industry peers, and co-workers.
e. Issues to be resolved.

Your diary can help you to:
- track your progress and analyze your own performance.
- become more aware of patterns which emerge in your daily selling experience.
- prepare selling strategies.
- prepare follow up strategies.
- give better marketing analysis to your builder.

CHAPTER THREE

Overcoming Objections

Chapter Two described how the **Strategy to Achieve Momentum** begins in the "first ten minutes." Of the eight stages of SAM, four begin during your initial interaction with your prospects — before they see a model home. Stage Five — "Lead the customer to pick out a favorite model" — involves product demonstration. Before I get to demonstration, I would like to detour from SAM for the next two chapters in order to discuss "Overcoming Objections" and "Creating Value." Understanding these two subjects will help the rest of your selling strategy to progress more smoothly by providing ways to keep your momentum alive when it becomes threatened. In Chapter Five I will return to product demonstration and then continue on through the remaining steps of the selling process.

Understanding the dynamics behind objections will give you insights for overcoming them.

You should never be intimidated by objections. They are simply one more part of the selling process to understand. You must understand the psychology behind objections, and how to overcome the different types which customers raise. Objections are handled by applying the same mentality which you have been developing in the first two chapters: understanding and fulfilling buyers' needs. Buyers have three types of needs: 1) Lifestyle, 2) Financial, and 3) Emotional. All three types of needs influence their homebuying decision.

There is a school of thought which says that objections should be avoided at all costs, and dismissed as quickly as possible when they arise. The goal of this approach is to elicit only positive responses, because that keeps the momentum going. If only life were so simple.

While positive responses are certainly good, negative responses can be just as good if you approach them with a positive attitude. Momentum doesn't have to come to a screeching halt when an objection arises.

Think of objections as feedback instead of obstacles.

Why do prospects raise objections? Understanding the motivation behind the objection will help you deal with it in a way which keeps momentum from stalling.

1. Sometimes prospects raise objections because they truly want no part of what you are selling. If you sense that this is the case, ask enough of the "Why?" types of questions so that at least you feel satisfied that you have identified their real needs. Once you feel that you understand those needs, then follow one of two courses:

    a) Redirect your strategy in terms of your new knowledge; or

    b) Let them go, and don't feel bad about it.

    You don't need to sell to everyone who walks in the door. A closing ratio of one in ten is generally considered outstanding. One in twenty is usually not bad. If you close one in ten, and your average weekly traffic is twenty, you will sell an incredible 104 homes per year. And even with such a dazzling record, you will still need to accept the fact that you will "lose" 936 prospects, and not let yourself get down about it.

2. Another reason that prospects raise objections is that they haven't yet figured out exactly what they want. In this situation, use the prospects' objections to help them, and you, to focus on identifying what combination of features will best meet their real needs.

3. Customers sometimes raise objections simply because they're scared. You need to be sensitive to the level of trau-

ma which the homebuying process arouses in many people. When you believe that the objection is more an expression of fear than of criticism, tell the customer about the experiences of other people like them who have bought from you. Occasionally you may also want to tell about people who did not buy, and later wish they had. Experiences of other people can go a long way toward increasing the comfort level of prospects who are frightened by the magnitude of the homebuying decision.

4. An objection may be a legitimate attempt to achieve a resolution which the buyer will not regret. In this situation the objection could actually be a sign of momentum rather than a blockade to it. The buyer is earnestly moving toward a buying decision, but is being cautious. Patience and sensitivity are the keys to dealing with this type of objection. Show your buyers that you care what is best for them, but also that you have the experience to help them. You have, after all, dealt with this same situation many times before, and have many satisfied customers to testify to the value of your expertise.

5. Sometimes objections are rooted more in psychological needs than in practical needs. Like the child who acts obnoxious just to get attention, some adults use objections more to express their need to feel important than to resolve specific issues. Again, patience and sensitivity can be tremendous assets to our selling success. While there's usually a voice inside us which responds to obnoxious objections by saying, "I don't need this," the truth is that some customers simply need to go through this emotional exercise. And some of them wind up being very grateful in the end to those salespeople who have the patience to put up with them.

These are five motivations behind objections. You may have encountered others. Try to deal with the objection in terms of its motivation whenever you can, and your chances of sustaining momentum will increase.

An objection does not always have to be resolved immediately.

Sometimes an objection will take you by surprise and you need time to think. Other times you need to get a better understanding of the objection before you respond. And in other situations the objection may be premature, and will work itself out if you can keep the buyer's attention for awhile longer. Sometimes it's OK to put an objection on the back burner, as long as you do not act as though you are dismissing the buyer's needs. For example, you might respond to your prospect's objection this way:

"I do want to address your question, because I know it's important to you. Can you hold on to your thought for a few minutes? I think you'll have the answer you need as soon as you see how it fits in with the other pieces of the puzzle."

This type of answer gives you time to think, or to learn more about the prospect's other needs. It also gives both you and the prospect time to evaluate the importance of his objection in the context of the other benefits which you are offering him.

An objection is not the same as a rejection. An objection may be nothing more than the prospect asking you to convince him that he is doing the right thing. Or it may be part of the subconscious battle for control of the selling environment which was introduced in Chapter Two.

I want to spend a little more time here digging into the mind of the buyer. In order to gain a true understanding of new home sales you need to stop from time to time and ask, "What is really going on here?" As was discussed in the last chapter, if you can understand some of the psychological dynamics in the buyer's motivations and responses, you can create more effective selling strategies.

One of these dynamics is the battle for control of the selling environment. And one of the elements in the battle for control of the selling environment is the battle for control of "territory" within the selling environment. As discussed earlier, controlling certain pieces of "territory" within the selling environment is like having the home field advantage in sports.

Establishing territory is one of the most subtle, yet critical dynamics in selling. The more you can keep the transaction in your territory, the better able you are to control your situation, sustain your momentum, and make the sale.

To describe what I mean by "territory," I will start with the basics.

What Is An Objection?

Most often an objection is *an unfavorable comparison in the prospect's mind between what his ideal is and what you are actually offering.*

The struggle for control of the selling environment is instinctive, not necessarily calculated. The salesperson wants control because he has a strategy to execute in order to do his job. The prospect is threatened by the natural tension which exists in a selling environment.

Think of a sale as a "contest." Instinctively that's what it is. Objections are part of the prospect's equipment in this contest. Your job in creating a non-threatening environment and raising the prospect's comfort level is to make it seem less like a contest, and more like a mutual effort to benefit the prospect. To reach into the prospect's mind, however, you still must understand that in the beginning there is a contest going on. The prospect instinctively attempts to control the selling environment by staking out a particular territory and making that territory the playing field for the contest. Go back to the definition of an objection: "an unfavorable comparison in the prospect's mind between what his ideal is and what you are actually offering." When a prospect raises objections to your product, the territory which he is staking out might be called "The Buyer's Ideal World."

One type of contest is what I call **Your New Home vs. the Other Real Alternatives.** *Fantasy is the buyer's territory; reality is yours.* You must claim your territory, and cause the contest to take place there.

Another territorial contest which you might encounter is what I will call **Your Total Package vs. Your Competitor's Individual Components.** Sometimes a prospect will zero in on one unfavorable aspect of your product, and then try to create a territory around that item. Or perhaps you are selling a product which doesn't have one really weak link. In that case the buyer might break the product down into its individual components, and attack one component at a time, rather than viewing the product as an integrated whole. This territory is frequently claimed by prospects when they want to negotiate. You cannot win on that field. You must transfer the transaction to your territory — "The Total Package." Your value lies in the complete package, not in your weakest link or your individual components.

Your Total Bottom-Line Value vs. Your Competitor's Discount is another example of a contest for territory. It can occur when you are competing against a builder who is "dealing." If your competitor is discounting or dealing by $10,000 and you are not, your prospect may claim that situation as his territory. The objection is that you will not deal as much as your competitor will (or you may not deal at all).

I will address these objection categories in detail, and give examples of how you can move the transaction from the buyer's territory into your own. Having the confidence to cause your buyers to re-evaluate their expectations is an important part of the selling process. Your goal is to make the contest occur on your home field, and the more effective you are at accomplishing this, the higher are your chances of winning. Approaching the sale with this mentality will take you a long way in your efforts to generate selling momentum.

Your Territory:
Your Home vs. The Other Real Alternatives

In order to deal with the objection which compares your product with the ideal world, you must first shift the buyer's mentality to the real world. The buyer must compare what you are offering to his current situation, and to what alternatives really exist in his price range. While your home may not seem to be exactly what the buyer thinks he wants, it may be closer to what he wants than anything else he can get in the real world. It may even be better than what he thinks he wants, once you have explained all the benefits of your home. Although your product may not meet all of the buyer's expectations, do not lose hope that your product may wind up meeting more of your buyer's needs than any of your competitors'.

Suppose your customer has picked out a favorite model, and you must now take him to see your lots. All of the lots which are now available back up to a two-lane suburban road. You know in advance that what you have to show will elicit an objection from almost every customer, and you know the customer will use this objection in a way that could threaten your momentum or your control of the selling environment. The best strategy as you enter this stage of the **Strategy to Achieve Momentum** is to attempt defusing the issue before the customer raises it.

For example, you might say, "We have two of the Berkley model available in our current section next to Central Avenue. People have liked that section, but we haven't sold them all." (Whether you use this approach will, of course, depend upon how many you have already sold in that section.)

Another approach might be, "Some people think they may not like this location when they first see it on the site plan because there's a road there. But once people actually see the lots, they've been very popular."

A third approach, especially if you are just releasing the section or have not sold any yet, might be, "We've just released our new section up by Central Avenue. I like these lots. I realize not everybody likes a home near a road, but someone who's really thought about it might prefer it, because there are some real advantages."

Some people might find this approach controversial. An opposing school of thought says you should never bring up an objection before the customer does. I disagree with this. If you're not sure whether you have a real objection, then I would agree, let sleeping dogs lie. But when you know, either from prior experience or from feedback, that the objection will arise (or worse still that the customer might think it but not express it, leaving the objection permanently unresolved), then you need to get into the buyer's mind before they develop their own prejudice. Otherwise you wind up on the defense. As the cliche goes, "the best defense is a good offense." In the chapter on "the first ten minutes," I discussed how important it is to get the prospect to see the product from your perspective. This principle is a critical element in controlling the selling environment, and is especially important with objections.

In each of the three examples of preparing the prospect to choose a lot backing up to a road, the salesperson showed the prospect that she was not trying to brush the objection off insensitively. She may have also generated some curiosity as to why someone would buy a home backing to a road. Of course, now that she has brought up the issue, she must be prepared to sell her position. The scenario below follows up on the salesperson's introductory remarks (whichever of the three she chose), and is designed to steer through the rough waters of the objection without losing momentum or control.

The salesperson arrives at the lots with the prospect.

Salesperson: "These are the two lots I was telling you about — lots 142 and 145. Personally I expect 142 to go first because of the color scheme. Lot 145 is the color you specifically said you didn't like, and most people feel the way you do. What do you think?"

Prospect: "I really don't like that road being back there."

S: "What it is that you particularly don't like?"

P: "There are actually three things that worry me. The noise, the privacy, and the lack of security."

S: "I understand what you're saying. I've heard other people say that, too. But do you know why people like these lots? Because when they stop and think about the other real alternatives, this stacks up better. Since the home itself meets your needs better than anything else you've seen, let me tell you how some other people have seen these lots with respect to your objections.

"First of all, about the noise. It's only a two-lane road, and while there is some traffic, the only time it's noisy is during rush hour. And at that point you're in your own car being part of it.

The other times it's just like it is right now, and the noise is not that bad. You might even want to stop by at a couple of different times of day to see what it's really like. I think you'll be pleasantly surprised at how quiet it is during evenings and weekends when you're at home.

"As for privacy, that's an interesting point. The next time a car comes into view around the corner, count the number of seconds it takes between the time you first see the car until the moment the car passes your home. Of course, once the car passes, the driver won't be able to see you any more unless he turns around."

[When a car appears, count out the seconds, or use your watch if possible. The more involved the prospect can be in this process, the better. Once the car has passed, then resume the conversation.]

S: "It was about three seconds. That means if the person in the car took all of his attention off of his driving and focused it on nothing but your home, even then the most he could see you is three seconds. That's not even enough time for most people to focus their attention. Which is really more private, this situation or the usual situation where your home backs up to another line of homes, with the same people there all the time, being able to watch you whenever they want?"

P: "That's an interesting point, but I think I'd rather wait for your section that backs up to trees. Is that you're next section?"

S: "It's not the next section, but the one after that. The next section backs up to other houses. The one after that backs up to trees, but since it's the only section with trees we'll have this year, we expect a fairly stiff lot premium."

P: "How much?"

S: "The builder hasn't decided yet. But there's another issue, and that's your point about security. If you were going to break into someone's home, would you break into a home backing up to trees where you could hide, or would you break into a home backing up to a public road where everyone can see you? Homes backing up to trees are not usually very popular with people who are concerned about security, and they cost more on top of that.

From what you've told me about other homes you've seen, Lot 142 is the best total combination of features which fit your priorities, especially at the price. Lot 145 would probably be second."

The approach which the salesperson has taken here ties together a number of important principles:

1. The salesperson does not talk down to the prospect or debate personal opinions with him. Instead she uses other buyers or prospective buyers as her point of reference. She backs up her points with third-party endorsements.
2. The salesperson displays patience, concern and empathy, and lets the prospect have his say. She does not then flippantly dismiss the prospect's objection as "not a problem," but tries to address the problem on the prospect's own terms. She keeps her focus on fulfilling the prospect's needs.
3. The salesperson puts the prospect's objection into the context of the other real, available alternatives. She builds on the fact that her home meets the buyer's other needs better than the other alternatives, and tries to put the objection into a more realistic perspective.
4. The salesperson employs both emotion and reason.
5. The salesperson creates urgency for the buyer not to lose Lot 142.
6. The salesperson allows the prospect to clearly articulate his objections. Many times, an objection becomes more manageable, and in fact shrinks once it is put into words.
7. The salesperson began to set up the objection as manageable, and elevated her own credibility, by addressing the objection positively and sincerely before the buyer did. She got the prospect to see the lots from her perspective.
8. The salesperson was able to sustain customer involvement through a) continuous interaction, b) addressing the customer's needs, c) bringing up the color scheme issue, and d) getting the customer involved in timing the car on the road.
9. The salesperson was able to inject subtle, tasteful humor into the conversation. Humor used properly can relax the customer and also show him that you are confident of your position.

10. The salesperson was able to make a favorable comparison between the situation which she is selling and the norm, showing that the objection could not only be tolerated, but could even be viewed as better than average.

In this example, the salesperson's goal was to maintain control and customer involvement by preparing for the objection and then meeting it head-on. She demonstrated that while what she was offering may not fit the prospect's preconceived ideal, it is still a better solution to the prospect's real needs than any of the real alternatives available in the prospect's price range. And it may even be better than the prospect's preconceived ideal.

She kept this portion of the transaction in her territory, rather than simply giving up and taking the prospect's name for the future section with the trees. She not only maintained her territory by selling "her home vs. the other real alternatives," but she also brought into play the next principle, selling "the total package."

Your Territory: The Total Package

You are selling *"an integrated, well-thought-out package, the whole of which is greater than the sum of its parts."* You are not selling "individual components." This is why concept selling is so important. It helps you to clearly establish your own territory earlier in the transaction.

You cannot always simply dismiss negative feedback as insignificant. But you can make a negative item compare favorably to the negatives of the other available alternatives. In the same way you can make your total package, as a balance of positives vs. negatives, compare favorably to the other available alternatives.

A number of individual components come together to make up your total package:
Location
Neighborhood
Quality of school system
Lot size, features and topography

Landscaping
Exterior architecture
Total livability of floorplan
Individual room sizes
Feeling and function of kitchen
Feeling and function of master bedroom suite
Innovation
Quality of construction specifications
Quality of detailing
Type of heating system
Reputation of builder
Warranty
Customer service
Sales track record of the project
Financing

When you receive objections in one or more of these areas, it is important to handle the objections one at a time with as much expertise as you can. It is equally important to relate a weakness in one particular area to the strength of your product as a whole. The value which the buyer obtains is measured in terms of most or all of the above items, not just in one or two. Most customers cannot afford a home which is strong in all of its components. What they need is the best balance of features — the best "total package" — for their money. You must make sure that while your buyers are raising objections to individual components, they are maintaining a big-picture mentality with respect to your product as a whole vs. the other available alternatives (including the home they live in now).

Your prospect may object to your kitchen in the following way:

"Most of the homes in this price range have an island in the kitchen and a larger eating space. The kitchen is really important to us because that's where we spend most of our time, and we can't see spending this kind of money and not even getting the kitchen we want."

Their objection is a legitimate one. It would be futile, and perhaps even insulting, to dismiss their objection as insignificant.

You could respond like this:

"I agree with you, the island kitchen is a nice feature, and most homes in this price range have one. But we felt it was smarter in the long run to use our space differently. We made the kitchen narrower so that we could line more cabinets and counter space along the wall, and also leave more space for a better entry foyer. Then we took a little space out of the eating area to put into the family room. There's still all the space you need for the eating area, and we didn't lose any function in the kitchen. Our customers have liked the fact that we were able to give them a nicer entry feeling and a larger family room than other homes in our price range. People have considered it an improvement."

Another type of objection might be this:

"Everyone but you offers crown moulding and chair rail as standard, and here it's an option. If you'll toss in those two things you've got yourself a deal. We're not really asking for any more than everyone else is giving, and we feel we're entitled to it."

Your response might be:

"Actually we already did toss it in, but we did it in the form of landscaping instead of crown moulding and chair rail. Since we've been offering it as an option, only one-third of our buyers have chosen it. But most people who have bought here have told us how much they appreciated the fact that we give the best landscaping in our price range. They say it proves we care about the look of the neighborhood as well as the homes themselves."

Selling the total package becomes particularly important in two situations:

1. When you're priced above most of your competition.
2. When you have a less desirable location than other alternatives in your price range.

In these two situations, you can't just trade off a few weak features with a few other stronger ones. You must go even farther in articulating the value of the total package. Again, selling the intelligence of your concept, and selling the features and benefits of your product as an integrated whole, become critical in establishing your total value.

A customer might say to you:

"These homes are $10,000 more than the ones at Oakview, and they're not that much larger."

Consider this response:

"You're right, and the homes at Oakview are very nice. But we have a different concept. We felt we could give you a home for just $10,000 more where you wouldn't have to make any concessions at all. I think you'll find the extra money is wisely spent. For only $80 a month more ($55 after taxes), you get sixty extra square feet in the family kitchen and fifty feet more in the master bedroom suite. The windows, cabinets and lighting fixtures are upgraded; our better landscaping package will make a better looking neighborhood; and we have a pool you can enjoy all summer. We've tried to create a better total lifestyle for as little extra money as possible. It may be a higher price, but we certainly believe it's a better value."

We see many examples of companies selling their total package in other industries. Mercedes emphasizes this strategy with their cars, while AT&T markets their "total package" of product, expertise, quality and service for "only pennies more" in the communications business. Neither of these companies sells price as their primary benefit. If you are at the bottom of your market in price and your product has broad market appeal, you may not always have to be as concerned about selling the total package. However, you still need to convince your buyers that they are not having to make more concessions than your lower price can justify.

A third type of contest for territory which I mentioned earlier was "Your Bottom-Line Value vs. Your Competitor's Discount." I will deal with this contest in detail in the next chapter — "Creating Value."

Summary

It is important to have a positive outlook to the whole subject of objections. "Objections are not the same as rejections." They do not necessarily hurt your momentum. In some cases, they can even help. It depends on why the objection is being made.

Don't stop the customer when he is raising an objection. Often the more thoroughly a customer can articulate an objection, the less significant the objection becomes. Once the objection can be reduced to words, it can not only be reasoned with, but it becomes more manageable and therefore diminishes.

I discussed five reasons why customers might raise objections.

1. It may be that your product is not right for your prospect. You won't sell to everybody. Even Ty Cobb, the best hitter in the history of baseball, didn't reach base half the time. A high percentage of failures was simply the nature of the game he chose to play. Despite all his "failures," he was still the best.
2. Some objections are made because the prospect doesn't really know what he wants yet.
3. Some are made because the prospect is scared.
4. Objections can be raised because the customer is legitimately trying to achieve an honest resolution.
5. Sometimes objections are rooted in psychological needs, such as the need for attention.

An objection becomes much more manageable when you realize that it is not insurmountable, and that you do not automatically lose when a customer raises an objection. Rather than viewing an objection as a reflection of a flaw in your product, view it as "an unfavorable comparison in the prospect's mind between what his ideal is and what you are actually offering."

Understand the dynamics behind objections. If you can deal with the dynamics, you can maintain control and momentum. Consciously or subconsciously, an objection involves a psychological struggle for territory between the buyer and the seller. This chapter discussed three types of territory which customers frequently try to stake out as the field on which the transaction is played:

1. "Their Ideal World."
2. "Individual Components" of your product.
3. "Your Competitor's Discount."

In these and other struggles for territory, you can sustain momentum through your "home court advantage."

Expect objections. It is difficult for many people to make an investment this large without raising some. They feel foolish if they do not. For the legitimate objections which you expect, plan your **Strategy to Achieve Momentum** so that it anticipates the objections and prepares the customer to view them from your perspective. Use third-party endorsements to boost your credibility in dealing with objections.

Action Items

1. Make a list of objections which you have had or anticipate at your project. After each one, provide at least one strategy for dealing with it. The elements of your strategy should include ;
    a) When to address the objection (before or after the customer brings it up).
    b) How to address it.
    c) A record of anecdotes or third-party endorsements which may strengthen your argument.
2. Continue to update this information as new situations arise.

Note: The purpose of this exercise is to prepare you with strategies for positioning your product favorably. As you develop this part of your preparation, be careful not to let your list of objections become demoralizing. All products have potential objections. Top salespeople succeed not because they encounter fewer objections, but because they handle objections more skillfully.

3. Know your competition well enough to be able to compare your total package with theirs if a prospect uses a competitor's product as leverage for his objection.
    a) Visit your competition.
    b) Keep their brochure, price list and option list on file.
    c) Keep notes on feedback from other prospects about your competitors' strengths and weaknesses.

Note: You will be building on this "action item" as part of

your preparation for "creating value" in Chapter Four. In this chapter the emphasis is on knowledge of your competition which is specifically relevant to overcoming objections. In the next chapter the emphasis will be expanded in order to develop a full understanding of your total value vs. that of your competition. Therefore, you may want to complete this "action item" at the same time you deal with the corresponding item at the end of Chapter Four.

CHAPTER FOUR

Creating Value

In Chapter Three I briefly mentioned "creating value" when I touched on the subject of selling against a discounting competitor. In this chapter I will explore the issue of value in greater detail, including strategies for competing against discounts.

You create value for your customer by providing more benefits for the money than anyone else. This approach to creating value includes two of the central themes of our **Successful Sales Mentality**:

1. Concept selling
2. Identifying and fulfilling the customer's needs

Like other components of your sales presentation, creating value starts with preparation.

1. Develop a knowledge of your market, paying particular attention to your most serious competitors. The primary information about your competition which you will need to track most closely includes:
   a. Sales rate
   b. Sales price
   c. Square footage
   d. Standard and optional items
   e. Lot features
   f. Amenities
   g. Financing

    h. Location advantages and disadvantages
    i. Particularly unique or noteworthy characteristics — positive and negative — about the product or community
2. Make a list of your product's primary strengths. (You listed its potential objections as one of your "action items" at the end of the last chapter.)
3. Highlight those strengths which are unique in your marketplace. They may be a part of your concept or your unique selling premise.
4. Write out your concept as you would articulate it in your "first ten minutes." (Refer back to Action Item #3 at the end of Chapter Two.) As stated earlier your concept includes:
    a. What you did.
    b. Why you did it.
    c. Who you did it for.
    d. What your results have been (if this information is advantageous or provable).

With these elements, your concept may sound something like this:

"Our goal at Timber Oaks was to put as much of our focus as possible into those parts of our homes which would be most important to our target market — folks like you. Our research told us that the parts of our homes which our market wanted to be outstanding were the family room and kitchen combination, the master bedroom and bath, and the exterior architecture. The market also told us they didn't want their money wasted on areas they rarely use — the living room, the dining room, the foyer and the fourth bedroom. What we learned was that if we really wanted to provide the best value to you and the best investment value for resale, we needed to make our priorities the same as our market's. That's what we did. The result is that buyers love these homes, and we've sold them faster than our most optimistic projections. We're very proud of Timber Oaks."

    5. Write out your "unique selling premise." This may be the same as your concept, it may be different, or it may overlap. It makes for a more consistent and less confusing presentation if your unique selling premise at least overlaps with

your concept. For example:
a. "We have more square footage in the family room and kitchen combined than any other community in our price range." Or,
b. "We're the only home in our location and price range to be recognized by *Professional Builder* magazine for our architectural design." Or,
c. "We're the best selling homes in our price range because our concept fulfills more of the market's needs than anyone else's. We just did what the market told us to do."
6. Write out why you would buy one of your homes. It may be because of the concept, or because of the unique selling premise, or because of something about the homes which excites you. Hopefully there would be many reasons. Be sure to make them part of your preparation, because it will strengthen your personal conviction and the power of your emotional selling. Emotional selling is critical to conveying value: the ability of a home — and a salesperson — to create excitement is just as much a part of its value as the home's price per square foot.

Value is always an important issue in the buyer's mind, whether it is being discussed at a particular moment or not. So make "creating value" a part of your "first ten minutes," and then keep reinforcing it through all the stages of SAM, right through the close.

Concept selling is not a substitute for product selling. It is an introduction to it. Establishing the concept allows you to establish the product's unique identity and credibility, and therefore is critical in creating its unique value. Your concept allows you to compete head-on with other products which are less expensive (or less expensive per square foot) without having to concede value.

Ultimately your concept is related to the sum total of your product's features and benefits, so the better you can articulate your product's features, benefits, and specific competitive advantages, the stronger your competitive position will be. Spend as much time with your production people and your purchasing people as you need in order to become a bona fide expert on your product. ***People want to buy new homes from experts.*** Unfortunately, very few new homes salespeople are true experts on their product, and the ones who are can wield far more power in their buyers' eyes through credibility. The competitive advantage alone is well worth the effort. The fringe benefit is that it will help keep you out of inadvertant misrepresentation problems.

Value is conveyed more convincingly through expertise than through any other form. If you have a favorable track record, that is your second most powerful weapon. Selling the builder is particularly important here, especially if your community or product line has no track record of its own. Make a list of your builder's achievements as part of your preparation. And if you have a personal track record of your own, use that as well. It will not only make you more believable, but your customer will know that you are working at your current project because you believe in it, and not because it's the only job you could get.

Dealing from a position of strength is another important element in creating value, especially when you are in a market where your competition is negotiating.

How do you deal from a position of strength if your project is not the best seller? Dealing from a position of strength is largely a state of mind. Another part of it is technical, and comes from simply knowing that you must deal from a position of confidence in order to instill in your buyers the confidence necessary for them to make a positive buying decision.

Emotional selling is one way to deal from a position of strength. Buyers respond to a salesperson's energy, activity, body language, and even voice variations. The salesperson's emotional enthusiasm for the product strengthens his position, as does his expertise.

Ironically, making the buyer feel good about himself does as much as anything to strengthen the salesperson's position. We all admire and listen to people who make us feel good about ourselves. Throughout the course of the transaction, there are a number of ways to make a buyer feel good about himself — perhaps even good enough to buy.

Creating Value

1. Give plenty of personal attention.
2. Remember specific personal things that they tell you about themselves.
3. Show genuine concern for their needs.
4. Show empathy, that you are able to identify with them.
5. Establish common ground.
6. Pay compliments.
7. Agree with and relate to their point of view.
8. Think of ways to make them feel smart, and confident about their ability to make good decisions, and then to act on those decisions.

Struggling to overcome a negative perception of value is one situation in which it seems very difficult to deal from a position of strength. A familiar example of this problem occurs when you have a competitor who is negotiating or discounting more than you are. This problem is worth discussing in detail.

Negotiating, Or Overcoming A Negative Perception of Value

Whether your prospect is objecting to your price, using the price of a competitor against you, or using the size of a competitor's discount against you, they are putting you in a position where you have to defend your value.

Appeal to the buyer's intelligence. In fact, flatter it. People frequently negotiate, or question value, because they would feel stupid if they didn't. Most buyers, even in sophisticated markets, are not savvy enough to discern total value in the new homes market, any more than they are in the new car market. They need to be told what standard to use as a basis for comparison. How do they know what builder is really giving the best price, or, in the case of a market where discounting is the norm, who is giving the best deal? What is the equalizer?

The market itself is the equalizer, and this is the message which you must convey clearly to your prospect. Here is one way to do it.

"Regardless of what any ad or salesperson tells you about what a generous deal they are giving you, the fact is that we are all selling our homes for as much as we can. That even includes us."

Begin with this honest approach, and you will capture your customer's attention. He believes he has been flim-flammed all day, and he wants just one person to tell him the truth.

"If our competitor is giving $10,000 off, there's only one reason he's doing it, and that's because he couldn't sell the home if he were offering $9000 off."

What you have accomplished here is to get the prospect back to square one, where you can start discussing your terms on your own territory, and not the territory of your competitor's discount or lower price. When we touched on this topic briefly in Chapter Three, we called the buyer's territory "Your Competitor's Discount." We called our territory "Total, Bottom-Line Value."

Keeping the discussion in your territory, you would continue by saying, "If our homes weren't worth what we're charging, people wouldn't be buying them. And if people buy them the first time, they'll buy them a second time, so you know your resale investment is strong here, too. When you're deciding which home is the best value, decide on the basis of which is best for you. Trust your own intelligence. That's all you need. Whatever you do, don't base your decision only on price. Price and value can be two very different things.

"Make your decision based on which home meets the most of your needs. From an investment standpoint, you can assume that if the home meets your needs, it will probably meet the needs of the person you sell to. The investment aspect of real estate really is that simple.

"Don't be fooled by deals. If a builder has to give a deal to sell a home, it only means he's admitting that the home isn't worth what he was charging in the first place. You have to assume you'll need to turn around and give the same deal when you resell it.

"When you buy a home, don't forget to think long-term. Whatever discount you get from anybody will be absorbed into your mortgage and become an amount so small that your next pay raise alone will pay for it many times over. By that time the deal will be part of your past, and the home will be your real life

Creating Value

and your future."

Again you are using an emotional sell to create value, but use intelligence as well. If your project has a solid sales record, that is a strong testimony to value. Make sure that every prospect who walks in your door knows it by the end of your first ten minutes.

Third-party endorsements are also very strong proof of value, especially if you have customers living in the community who are willing to recommend you to prospects in person, or to provide quotes for you to display in your sales office.

Understanding exactly how your builder spends his money can also help you to highlight areas of value to your customers which they might otherwise not notice on their first visit to your community. If your builder put $1200 extra into windows or $400 extra into an air infiltration prevention system, make sure your customers realize that this expense provides them a better quality of life.

Flatter your customers' ability to see both the total picture and the specific benefits of your value vs. the value of your discounting competitor. Make sure your customers are comparing your competitor's bottom-line value with your bottom-line value, not just their discount vs. yours. Your competitor's discount is an insult to your customers' intelligence, and it is that intelligence which must become your ally. Your customers must be able to see past the deals in order to make the most intelligent homebuying decision.

In some way, nearly every product offers some form of value which its competitors do not. Unfortunately, in some products that "something special" is more obscure than in others. Sometimes your value is difficult to justify by merely "comparing apples with apples." If you happen to be selling a product with several strong features but a weak overall concept, then sell value by finding as many features as possible in your homes which other builders do not include. Use these features as "symbols" of your product's overall superiority.

Whatever your value advantage may be, make sure you articulate it clearly in your "first ten minutes."

When customers attempt to negotiate, they generally have three needs which you must fulfill in order to satisfy them.

1. They want to know they got the best price possible.

Tell the customer that you know that if you did not give him the best deal possible, he would never buy your home. You really want him to buy your home, so you'd be a fool not to give him the best deal you can.

In many cases the customer has already decided he wants to buy your home by the time he begins to negotiate. But if he continues to demand the best deal possible, ask him, "How will you know when you have gotten the best deal possible?" This is, of course, a very difficult question to answer, and it forces the customer to tell you the argument he wants you to use on him in order to convince him.

2. They want a sense of victory.

Make sure your customer understands the difference between a discount and a value. The buyer's victory is achieved when he gets the best home and the best value, not the best discount. The best discount could very well come with the worst home, or the worst value. Often that is, in fact, exactly why it requires the biggest discount.

3. They believe that when they get a discount on a new home, they are making money.

Again, if this were true the seller would not need to be discounting in the first place. Explain to the customer that "every builder sells his homes for the highest price he can. Discounting is just one more artificial strategy for creating urgency. Assume that whatever discount you get from your seller, you will have to then pass on to your buyer, in one form or another."

The Spirit of Negotiation

In markets where negotiating is not normal in new home sales, market slowdowns which do cause negotiating are particularly disheartening. We are neither emotionally nor technically equipped to handle it. We believe that when buyers ask for something, the only way we can make a sale is to give it to them.

After all, it's a buyer's market, and they mean business, and they're not going to buy unless they get exactly what they want.

Beware of this mindset. It is crippling and self-defeating.

In negotiation, no one ever gets everything he wants. If he did, it wouldn't be a negotiation. A good negotiator maintains the mindset that a negotiation is successful when:

1. Everyone believes the deal makes sense for them.
2. Everyone believes the deal is fair.

Regardless of their blustering, people in negotiations rarely expect to get everything they ask for. Salespeople in certain other businesses understand this better than we do in new home sales. Buyers simply get to the point where they stop asking for more. Sometimes in fact, when buyers do get everything they ask for it can actually increase their chances of getting buyer's remorse, or a desire to renegotiate, later.

Maintaining a position of strength is critical in negotiating, as it is in creating value. You must not allow "the tail to wag the dog" by letting negotiation become a primary issue at the beginning of the transaction. You should continue through your game plan —SAM — and address the customer's need to negotiate as close to the end of the transaction as possible. If the customer continues to press you to negotiate earlier, you must explain to him that negotiation will have no meaning until he understands exactly what he is getting for his money. Once he understands what the total value is, you will address the negotiation as earnestly as you can.

Your goal in a negotiation must be to:

1. Articulate and reinforce your value, through both emotional and rational selling, to the point where the buyer believes the purchase makes sense for him.
2. Convince the buyer that the deal is fair.
3. Convince the buyer that you gave him the best deal you possibly could.

Summary

One study designed to measure buyer's motivations concluded

that customers rate major factors in their buying decision in the following order of importance:
1. Location
2. Community
3. Product design
4. Auxiliary components (kitchen, bath, family room, etc.)
5. Price and terms

While other studies have drawn different conclusions, the point to be made here is that price should not be sold as the most important factor in the decision process. Too often the list above is sold in reverse.

Price is not the same as value. Value is the sum of the five factors listed above, plus many more. Your goal is to sell value, not price. You create value for your customers by "providing more benefits for the money than anyone else can."

To sell value you must:
1. Know your competition.
2. Know your product's strengths.
3. Know which of those strengths are unique in the marketplace.
4. Sell your concept.
5. Sell your unique selling premise.
6. Be able to say with conviction why you would buy one of your homes.

As in overcoming objections, you sell value in terms of your total package. Your buyers must compare your total package against the other available alternatives.

Creating value requires you to maintain a position of strength. There are several ways to maintain your position of strength throughout the selling process:
1. Sell your expertise (which includes knowledge of your product and your competition).
2. Focus on your total package and your product's strengths.
3. Employ emotional selling.
4. Keep the buyer's level of confidence high by making them feel good about themselves.
5. Sell your track record if you have one.

6. Use third-party endorsements.
7. Delay the negotiating aspect of the transaction as far into SAM as possible.

Defend yourself against price-cutting competitors by explaining to your customers that they should not be fooled by deals: everyone always sells their homes for as much as they can get. The market is the true equalizer of value. Make sure your buyers focus on total value and take a long-term perspective for their own good.

To complete a successful negotiation, you do not necessarily have to give your buyer everything he wants. But you must satisfy your buyer that:
1. The purchase makes sense for him.
2. The deal is fair.
3. You gave him the best deal you could.

Action Items

1. Return to the first page of this chapter and prepare a summary of your competitors, including information on the items listed, plus other items which are of particular importance in your market. If your company does not already provide you with a standardized form for this type of analysis, you might want to develop one of your own.

Note: This item is a continuation of Action Item #3 in Chapter Three.

2. List as many elements of your product as you can think of which will help you to sell superior value. These elements may include:
    a. Concept
    b. Unique selling premise
    c. Location advantages
    d. Architectural and design features
    e. Square footage/room sizes
    f. Construction features
    g. High quality interior items
    h. Lot features

      i. Community features and amenities
      j. Sales success
      k. Awards or other recognition
      l. Other achievements by your builder
      m. Third-party endorsements
      n. Financing

3. Write out a list of reasons why you would buy one of your homes.

Note: This list may overlap with the items in #2, but it is worth the separate exercise in case you think of additional items which appeal to you personally but are not on the list above.

4. List all of your competitors who you believe are discounting or negotiating more than you are. If you do not have any evidence that you are actually losing sales to them *because of their discounting strategy,* then dismiss their negotiating as a potential threat to you. Often a discounting strategy does have little impact on the sales rate of its competitors. But if you do believe that you are losing sales to a discounting competitor, then write out your own strategy for demonstrating that you are still providing a better value than they are. Use the information which you prepared in Action Items 1-3 above.

5. List all of your competitors who are outselling you. Again using the information from Action Items 1-3, develop a strategy to show ways in which you offer superior value to each of them specifically.

Note: Each of these five Action Items has a slightly different orientation for creating value. The combination of all five items will provide you with a complete perspective of your product's highest value. It will also produce an index of information which will enable you to demonstrate your value favorably in the variety of situations which require strong value selling.

CHAPTER FIVE

Demonstrating Your Product

Understanding the dynamics of "overcoming objections" and "creating value" will help you to sell more effectively once you get beyond your initial interaction with the prospect in your sales office. I will now pick up where I left off at the end of Chapter Two and continue with the **Strategy to Achieve Momentum**.

In the "first ten minutes" you initiated the first four stages of SAM:

1. Establish Rapport.
2. Sell your concept.
3. Determine your customer's needs.
4. Begin to set the stage for showing that your product fulfills those needs.

At this point you move from your sales office into your model homes (or whatever you use to demonstrate your product if you don't have a model). Product demonstration leads you from stage four to stage five of SAM:

5. Lead the buyer to pick out a favorite model.

If you can accomplish this stage, your momentum will be accelerating and you can begin focusing on your strategies for the last three stages:

6. Lead the customer to pick out a favorite lot.
7. Create in the customer's mind the fear of losing that lot.
8. Ask for the order.

Product demonstration is therefore frequently a turning point in the selling process.

Demonstrating your product adds an entire dimension to your presentation — the third dimension. A sales office is primarily two-dimensional — lines, words and pictures on flat displays. They are things you look at. A model home (or a house under construction if you are selling without models) is something which surrounds you.

Raising emotions is much easier in a three-dimensional setting than in a two-dimensional one. An important part of selling is "show and tell," and you can show in a model what you can only tell about in a sales office. An additional benefit of product demonstration is that your prospect's feedback during this phase of the sale can be one of your most important sources of momentum.

Tremendous opportunities to create excitement and momentum through product demonstration are lost on the grounds that "the customer didn't want me to go with them." Sometimes customers really don't want you to go with them, and in some of those situations it would do more harm than good to accompany them. Nevertheless, I have been amazed by the number of top salespeople who really do accompany most of their buyers through the models because they believe it is essential to their effectiveness. These salespeople also get surprisingly little resistance.

As they conclude their first ten minutes, they use a variety of approaches to introduce the subject of accompanying the prospect through the models.
1. "We have three models for you to see. Let me get you started in the first one by showing you what's standard and what's optional, so it will be easier when you're walking through the other two."
2. "I've given you a brief overview of our concept and our community here in the sales office. Let me show you a couple of highlights in the homes themselves."
3. "I'd love for you to see our models. Would it be all right if I go through the first one with you? I know a lot of people

prefer to go along without a salesperson tagging along, but I'd appreciate the opportunity to point out a few things that we're really proud of."

Going through the effort of demonstrating models can go a long way in deepening your relationship with your customer, and in strengthening the customer's loyalty to you. If you find the idea of demonstrating models intimidating because you think you are intruding upon the prospect, then think of demonstrating as a service rather than as a selling technique. The buyer really does stand to benefit from your demonstration, and so do you.

There are as many styles of model demonstration (and of making the transition from sales office to model demonstration) as there are salespeople. Even top salespeople have different degrees of comfort in breaking out of the sales office with their customers. The important thing is not to let the sales office become your cocoon. Tremendous time and effort went into the planning of every detail of the homes, and a lot of money may have been spent merchandising them. It still takes an enthusiastic demonstration to bring these assets to life. Like a cook who spends six hours preparing a Thanksgiving dinner which is devoured by the guests in thirty minutes, the salesperson needs to help moderate the buyer's pace so that the feast may be savoured and appreciated. The typical customer who's in a hurry to see as many different projects as he can between 11:00 and 6:00 often does not have the mindset necessary to discern for himself why your product is better than your competitors'. Nor does he have the motivation to uncover many of the more subtle benefits of your homes' features. Some of your most significant features may not be noticeable — or even visible — in the models, and therefore require verbal explanation along the way.

Top salespeople claim that their most productive selling time is in the models and on the site showing lots, not in the sales office. They devote the sales office to the first ten minutes — establishing initial rapport — and to the final paperwork. They do their actual selling outside the sales office, where they can bring their product to life and create more customer involvement.

You have four primary goals in demonstrating models or homes under construction:
1. To develop a deeper relationship with your customer, learn more about their individual needs, and establish greater credibility.
2. To bring your concept to life, and to allow the customer to more fully understand the features and benefits of your homes.
3. To shift your emotional selling into a higher gear by:
   a. showing personal enthusiasm, and
   b. selling the customer a better quality of life.
4. To get your customer to pick out a favorite model, in order to keep them progressing toward your next stage of SAM.

During your "first ten minutes," you are developing rapport and creating an atmosphere which makes prospects more comfortable with your presence as they prepare to see the models. You do this by positioning yourself as non-threatening, as an expert, and as a counselor (or "assistant buyer") instead of a seller. If you succeed in establishing this kind of rapport with your prospects, then you will probably have succeeded in increasing their comfort level to the point where they believe you can do them more good than harm by going through the models with them.

Remember that one of the fundamental principles of SAM is that in every stage of the sequence you are laying the foundation for the next stage. In the first ten minutes you are positioning yourself to continue your relationship with the prospect beyond those minutes and into the models. Phrases like "I'll show you what I mean in a few minutes," or "I'll be interested to see what you think of our concept when you see it brought to life in the models," can help plant the seeds for a smooth transition.

Once again preparation builds a tremendous advantage. Prepare a list of those features and benefits which you want to highlight, as well as the questions you want to ask your prospects as you take them through.

Some salespeople plan to only accompany their prospects through one model, and then let them see the remaining one(s) alone. They feel that the job of demonstration can be adequately accomplished in one model, and believe that giving the prospect a little time away from the salesperson is good after a point. You need to gauge that situation for yourself on a case-by-case basis. If the customers seem willing for you to continue with them, then I would certainly not back off. One of the principles of "aggressive selling" which has already been discussed is that the salesperson is never the one who causes the momentum to stop.

Another time to continue through additional models is when your prospect's responses lead you to believe that one of your other homes would appeal to him. Never forfeit a chance to take your best shot. Seeing additional models always gives you a chance for more interaction, more feedback, more involvement and more selling. Prospects are more likely to open up in the model homes than in the sales office, but going through all the models with the prospect is sometimes too threatening. Each situation therefore requires an on-the-spot judgment call.

One of the most basic rules in selling any product is, "Sell benefits, not features," or, "Sell the sizzle, not the steak." Of course, in reality you are selling both the feature and the benefit, the sizzle and the steak. The sizzle has no value if you cannot convince the customer of the quality of the steak. A technical description of the feature sells knowledge, which the customer needs. He needs the information as well as the sense of security which grows out of his confidence in you, your builder and your product. Selling the benefit usually has even greater impact than selling the feature: the benefit brings the feature to life and gives it value by relating it to the customer's needs. Fulfilling needs is the key to controlling the selling environment and sustaining momentum.

You can increase your impact in selling benefits by relating positive experiences of other people who have bought. Both of the following statements are strong, but I believe the second is stronger.

1. "You'll love this sunroom all year round, but especially in the autumn and spring."
2. "People who live here have told me again and again how

much they love this sunroom. They use it all year round, but they love it most in autumn and spring. They say that being able to spend more time out in the spring and fall weather really makes life more enjoyable."

Third-party endorsements (even general ones) make the statement that your homes have improved the lives of other people who have the same kinds of needs as your prospects'. As part of your preparation for this segment of your presentation, keep in touch with your customers after they have moved in, and get to know the ways they are using and enjoying their new homes. Use these types of anecdotes to help enhance your emotional selling. Also, let your prospects know your own positive feelings about the product. Even though you're obviously the salesperson, you're also human, and you can humanize yourself by expressing your personal responses.

Make sure your model demonstration does not degenerate into a monologue. As in other parts of the transaction, you want to use every opportunity to listen and learn. Even simple questions like "What do you think of this family room?" or "Have you seen any other kitchens like this for under $200,000?" can help you to see how you're progressing. If it is appropriate to ask more in-depth questions like "Does this home have the type of floorplan you're looking for?" then so much the better. Remember the principle, ***If you ask the right questions and then listen carefully enough, your prospects will tell you how to sell them a home.***

Throughout your demonstration, attempt to elicit responses concerning optional items, color selections and alternate exteriors — non-threatening issues which allow your prospect to express preferences. Making those secondary decisions helps the customer to become more involved in your homes and provides an additional means of generating the type of momentum which can be directed toward a close.

Use your model demonstration to create value, and to reinforce your concept and your unique selling premise. As discussed in the last chapter, understanding how your builder spent his money will help you articulate to your prospects the benefits which they will be getting for theirs.

Some of these benefits will not be obvious to your customers. Selling the hidden benefits is a particularly important element of your model demonstration. It ties together your expertise with your product's value. It also shows your customers values which they would not have realized on their own, and may help them to identify needs which they didn't even know they had.

Include technical construction explanations in your presentation. If your prospects seem bored by them, you don't have to bend their ears, but at least you showed them that your expertise is there if they need it. This effort will help to raise you and your builder to a higher level of credibility than your less-informed competition. As stated earlier, people want to buy from experts. Given a preference, a customer would normally rather buy from a "builder" than from a "salesperson," because they consider the builder to be the expert. So the more you can do to represent yourself as having a builder's knowledge and perspective, the higher you will raise your customer's comfort level.

As discussed in the chapter on "Creating Value," buyers are often motivated by displays of energy and action. Activity creates involvement, and raises the emotional level. Be animated, and vary your voice level so that you are not speaking in a monotone.

Keep your eye contact focused on your buyers, as opposed to walking in front of them and talking in the opposite direction.

Use your hands to help create an animated demonstration, as opposed to folding your arms or putting your hands in your pockets.

Take advantage of the three-dimensional advantages of model demonstration by making sure that prospects walk into a room, as opposed to just peering through the doorway.

Don't be content with merely describing what your product is. Describe what it can be for your customer. Creating visions is a vital element in emotional selling. It helps bring the product to life in a personal way, tailored to the buyer's needs. Creating visions is what raises selling from being solely a craft to being an art as well. Again, use the gratifying experiences of other buyers to help you create these visions.

Third-party endorsements also help you to sell the neighbors themselves. It is important for your prospects to feel that they will enjoy their neighbors. Neighborhood and location should be sold and reinforced at every point possible.

The climax of your efforts in model demonstration occurs when your prospect picks out a favorite model. The purpose of your demonstration is to achieve stage four of SAM — showing that your product fulfills your prospect's needs better than his current situation, and better than any of the other available alternatives. While the *purpose* of your demonstration is to achieve stage four, the ultimate *goal* of your demonstration is to achieve stage five — leading them to pick out a favorite model. It is important not to move too quickly toward this goal, because when the buyer makes his selection, it should be with conviction. It is also important that you keep sight of this goal throughout the demonstration process.

Your ability to get your prospects to focus on a particular model is crucial in generating the momentum necessary to get them to the next all-important stage — picking out a favorite lot.

Summary

The **Successful Sales Mentality** views model demonstration as a service, and not merely as a sales technique.

Effective product demonstration gives you a significant edge over those competitors who are less enthusiastic about this stage of the selling process.

1. It provides a better environment for emotional selling.
2. It allows you to more effectively identify and fulfill your customer's needs.
3. It enables you to sell more competitively, highlighting features of your homes which are better than your competition.
4. It gives you an opportunity to deepen your relationship with your customer.
5. It helps to raise your customer's comfort level by enabling

you to show superior expertise, as well as a more caring attitude than other salespeople.

6. It provides an opportunity for you to gather more feedback.

Product demonstration must be energetic as well as enthusiastic. Buyers respond to energy and animation.

Use your models to bring your concept to life, as well as to sell features and benefits. Combining these two objectives will give you an additional advantage in creating value. Take advantage of this extra time with the customer to listen and learn, as well as to sell.

Create customer involvement through questions designed to elicit responses requiring involvement: questions like how your customer might personally use an area or function, or which options would benefit the customer.

Be sure to sell benefits which may be hidden from the customer's view.

Use models (or spec homes if there are no models) not only to demonstrate tangibles, but also to help your customers create their own visions.

Stay focused on the ultimate goal of getting the customer to pick out a favorite model so that you can begin to create urgency. Then be prepared for the next stage of SAM — getting the customer to pick out a favorite lot.

Action Items

1. Write out one or more ways in which you can comfortably set yourself up to accompany your prospects through at least one model.
2. Make a list of features and benefits which you want to demonstrate in at least the first model, and prepare how to demonstrate them with maximum impact.
3. Make a list of qualifying questions and need-identification questions to ask your customers as you accompany them through your model.
4. Make a list of third-party endorsements which will help make your demonstration more effective.

5. Decide how you are going to get them to tell you which model they like best so that you can begin to focus on taking them to your available lots.

CHAPTER SIX

Showing Lots

For many top salespeople, showing lots is the most exciting stage of the selling process. It includes two critical stages in the **Strategy to Achieve Momentum:**

Stage 6 — Lead the customer to pick out a favorite lot.

Stage 7 — Create in the customer's mind the fear of losing that lot.

This is the point in the sequence where your momentum accelerates most quickly. In this respect, showing lots may be considered the true climax of the selling process. It is the stage which brings together the strategies of the **Successful Sales Mentality** which we have developed up to this point, and it is the stage which sets up the close. Successfully executed, stages 6 and 7 of SAM lead naturally and comfortably to the final stage:

Stage 8 — Ask for the order.

One of the advantages of a carefully planned and thoroughly executed **Strategy to Achieve Momentum** is that by the time you get to Stage 8, it is the easiest part of the sale.

There are four elements of the **Successful Sales Mentality** which you must focus on throughout the process of showing lots — from the moment you take your prospect to the lots until the moment you ask for the order. Think of these four elements as "themes" — or purposes — which run throughout your lot-showing strategy.

1. *You are creating a vision with your prospect.* The most cre-

ative aspect of selling is leading your prospects to visualize themselves in one of your homes. You are helping them to create their dream, and to take the steps necessary to fulfill that dream. You have learned the prospect's needs. Now you are helping them to envision a life in the near future in which those needs have been met.

2. *You are selling the community.* Part of the vision mentioned above is the home itself. Another part is the neighborhood to whom the buyer will belong. For many people, this part of the vision is even more important than the home itself.

3. *You are selling your company's expertise* in design, construction and development. You are also *selling your own expertise* in the process.

4. *You are creating urgency.* You are showing them that there is one particular home and lot which is better for them than any other, and that they will have to take action in order to prevent someone else from getting it first.

While keeping these four purposes as part of your focus in showing lots, you must also understand ten of the critical dynamics, — or characteristics — of this phase of the selling process. Understanding these ten principles will help you to move through stages 6 and 7 of SAM, and into stage 8. They overlap logically with the four purposes listed above, and they will make this phase of the selling process very powerful.

The Ten Dynamics of Showing Lots

1. Emotional selling
2. Creative selling
3. Bringing the transaction to life
4. Controlling the selling environment
5. Increasing customer involvement
6. Enhancing your credibility
7. Selling the neighborhood
8. Choosing a favorite lot
9. Creating fear of loss

10. Beginning the close

Prior to taking your prospects to any lots, it is ideal if you have already determined which model is their favorite. Occasionally it is impossible for them to choose a favorite model until they have seen the lots. They might have two or more models that they like, and the actual homesite may be the deciding factor. Generally, however, it is easier if they have already picked out their favorite model, including the elevation. You should also know why the model is their favorite so that you will be able to reinforce their positive feelings if objections arise or if the momentum seems to be slowing down. Also you will also be using the accumulation of their positive feelings in the close.

I will now examine each of these selling dynamics in detail, and show how to maximize the effectiveness of each.

1. Emotional Selling

I have discussed emotional selling in previous chapters. In showing lots, emotional selling manifests itself in the following ways:

    a. Your own personal enthusiasm for the lots and homes you are showing.

The technical part of your demonstration, or tour, should be no less enthusiastic than the creative, visionary part.

    b. Individualizing and personalizing your tour.

Your focus is still on fulfilling your prospect's needs, which you have learned during the first ten minutes and during the product demonstration. This stage in the sequence is also another opportunity to refine your understanding of the prospect's needs. Probing for those needs is frequently easier, now that you are dealing with more specific information. As you get into one specific detail after another, you can elicit feedback from the prospect in order to help you stay on track.

    c. Creating customer involvement (which goes hand in hand with "a" and "b").

    d. Creating urgency.

This results after "a," "b," and "c" have been successfully accomplished. Once urgency has been created, SAM proceeds automatically to the closing stage.

2. Creativity

What do we mean when we talk about "helping the customer to create a vision of their new home?" It means much more than simply taking a customer to a lot with only a foundation in the ground and saying, "Imagine yourself living here someday."

Creating a vision in new home selling involves a combination of artistic and technical skills.

Suppose you are taking your prospect to a lot on which construction has not yet started. In fact, even grading has not yet been completed. The tools you need to take with you are a site plan, an engineer's ruler and a 100-foot tape. Standing on the lot, you explain how the lot will slope, how drainage will work, where and how the home will be sited. Keep the prospect involved by such means as allowing him to hold one end of the tape or standing at a particular corner of the lot while you demonstrate its size.

The brochure may be adequate in this situation for representations concerning the product. If it is not, then you should also take along the blueprints of the home, with an architect's ruler.

This is the *technical* aspect of creating a vision. It adds substance, credibility and understanding to the vision.

You exercise your *artistic* expertise as you begin verbally painting your picture with your customer, using whatever visual props you have at your disposal: the brochure, construction drawings, or other homes nearby.

As in product demonstration, focus on selling benefits as well as features. There are many elements which may become a part of your vision. Here are a few of them:

   a. views
   b. trees
   c. future landscaping
   d. house siting
   e. product features which relate to the lot (sunroom, deck, garage, windows, doors, basement entry, etc.)
   f. lot size and usability

g. privacy
h. accessibility
i. maintenance advantages
j. neighbors

Relate your verbal painting to needs which your customer has already articulated, and to competitive advantages which you have over other available options in the marketplace. Without this focus, the most eloquently expressed vision may not necessarily create customer involvement or urgency. Give credibility to your vision with examples of how it appeals to others, or to you personally.

As with other components of your selling program, preparation — one lot at a time — will give you a great head start, and a tremendous advantage over your competitors who are unwilling to make this effort.

3. Bringing the Transaction To Life

As you help the customer to create his vision, you allow him to move closer to the reality of actually owning the home. The salesperson who shies away from this approach cannot create the same involvement, excitement and momentum.

Your goal in bringing the transaction to life is to increase the prospect's comfort level with the possibility of buying. You want to show the prospect that buying a new home is not merely some remote possibility that is light years away from reality. Many prospects fail to buy because the idea of buying is truly inconceivable to them. Not only is it intimidating, it simply isn't real. It is an idea which they have grown to associate with fantasy.

Your greatest asset in turning their fantasy into reality is the fact that you have done it before. Retrieve those experiences and expose the prospect to them. Buying a home is much more normal, and easier, than most people think. You know it because you sell to these people all the time. Without being insensitive to the prospect's trauma, you can still show him that other buyers fight the same trauma and overcome it, and benefit tremendously when they do. It is easier to convey this perspective on the actual site, where the homes of other people, just like your prospect, stand as evidence of dreams fulfilled.

Why should your customer remain stuck in a home which he has already admitted is unsatisfactory while other people improve their lives because they have a better understanding of how easy it is? In most housing markets it is harder for a purchaser to make a mistake that he cannot fix than it is with virtually any other major purchase or investment (reselling the home being the worst-case scenario). People's understanding of this basic principle has helped them to make the good decisions necessary to improve both their lives and their financial well-being.

4. Controlling The Selling Environment

Showing lots provides opportunities for you to gain more control over your selling environment than you have been able to achieve in any previous stage of the selling process. There are several reasons for this:

   a. Your prospects have already implicitly agreed to relinquish a certain amount of control by agreeing to let you take them away from the sales office and out to a lot. They realize that they are expressing a small degree of commitment. This is the most threatening step yet in the transaction for them. By taking it they are acknowledging a level of trust and rapport, and they are expressing a willingness to develop the relationship, and to pursue their buying objective even further. They realize that they are much more your "prisoner" out on the job site than they were in your sales office or your model homes. And yet they have given their consent to these conditions.

One of the characteristics of SAM is that each stage which you achieve requires the prospect to relinquish more control of the selling environment to you. This helps keep your strategy on track. It also accelerates your momentum until some new event or thought process causes the momentum to stall.

When the momentum does stall, it is important that you not necessarily consider it a failure. While there may come a point in SAM where the prospect decides that buying your home is absolutely out of the question, there are other times when SAM simply needs to pause for awhile, like an engine which has overheated. But it must always be the customer, and never the salesperson, who decides that SAM needs to pause. Remember our definition of aggressive selling: "continuing through the stages of SAM until the customer causes you to stop."

Once your momentum has stalled, your goal is to find an appropriate moment to pick up where you left off and regenerate the momentum. This moment may occur later during the same visit, or it may be at a future time. The important thing is not to let stalls in your momentum discourage you from continuing to pursue SAM with your next customer. Your goal cannot be focused solely on achieving a close every time. This type of all-or-nothing mentality can become very discouraging. It might cause you to give up, or to take short cuts prematurely. Instead your goal should be to get as far as you can with SAM every time, knowing that a healthy ratio of closes will be your reward.

If you can get one out of every five prospects who walks in your door to the point where they allow you to show them at least one lot, and if you can then close one out of every three people to whom you show a lot, you would still have the healthy closing ratio of one in 15.

  b. Another reason you can increase control of your selling environment by showing lots is that you get the prospect out of a strictly business environment and into a more casual one. While showing lots could potentially be a more threatening phase of SAM than any previous phase, it often turns out to be more enjoyable, and even exciting. This is because the atmosphere is more relaxing, and often more adventurous. It is important to awaken your prospect's sense of adventure as you show lots. The more relaxing and adventurous atmosphere often stimulates more meaningful conversations between you and your prospect. As much as possible, take advantage of this benefit of the lot-showing experience.

  c. Showing lots gives you a long period of uninterrupted time with the prospect. No telephones. No other customers. And again, prospects are more likely to allow you to set the pace of the interaction in the field than they were in the sales office. Even though prospects are not likely to walk away from you out in the field, be sensitive to their comfort level and sense of time. If you see signs of agitation, it could mean you are talking too much and that the prospect is desiring a change in the tempo of your tour. It is very easy for a salesperson to become inadvertantly dominant during the lot-showing stage, and this is one sure way of stalling momentum, or reducing your prospect's comfort level.

5. *Increasing Customer Involvement in Your Product*

During the model demonstration you articulated features and benefits of the home, and attempted to relate as many as possible to the prospect's individual needs. While showing lots you revisit these features and benefits: now you are applying them to a specific home on a specific lot. Since the prospect has already expressed discontent with his current situation, this is also a time to revisit his discontent, and to remind him that purchasing this one particular home (stressing its uniqueness) is a truly positive step in his life.

This is a stage where it is important to pursue your customers' needs and satisfaction with diligence, but not to beat them over the head with it. Remember, customers always know what you're up to, and a hard-sell approach at this particular moment can cause your prior efforts in building trust and rapport to suddenly unravel. You are recalling their needs and their earlier positive responses to your product in order to show your attentiveness and care, not to beat them into submission.

6. *Enhancing Your Credibility*

Showing lots gives you an advantage not only in selling your product, but in selling your builder and yourself as well. As you explain details of construction, engineering and land planning, you create an intellectual involvement on the part of the buyer which adds a dimension to their emotional involvement. With some purchasers, intellectual involvement will ignite emotional involvement. The more knowledge they gain, the more excited they become.

Again, people want to buy from experts, especially when they are seeking assurances of quality. Don't just assure your prospect that he will have a dry basement. Explain grading principles which relate to drainage, as well as relevant construction features such as parging and drain tile. Show them how their window wells or exterior basement stairwells will drain. Explain the difference between a wet basement and condensation. And let the customer know the maintenance aspect of keeping a basement dry (maintaining a positive grade away from the home around the foundation, keeping gutters clean, etc.). These kinds of detailed explanations increase customer involvement in addition to increasing your own credibility.

Taking your customers through homes in various stages of construction will enable you to sell more of the construction benefits of your product. It will also show your customers that you are willing to commit your time to giving them the attention and care that they need. By making them realize that they are special to you, you help strengthen your emotional bond with them. The emotional bond becomes increasingly important in big-ticket items such as jewelry, cars, insurance, and, of course, homes. By investing your time, effort and care in your prospects, you create not only a bond, but sometimes a type of "emotional indebtedness." While people are not likely to buy a home they don't want out of emotional indebtedness to the salesperson, this indebtedness is still an advantage, and is a critical part of emotional selling.

As you show homes in various stages of completion to demonstrate construction benefits, include homes which are nearly completed in order to show your pride in your company's finished product. This can also help you to overcome the customer's skepticism that the true quality of your home has been obscured by model decorating. (Naturally, the cooperation of your construction department is essential to your ability to sell the quality look of a nearly finished home.) Showing your customers a nearly finished home will enable you to begin imagining, with these customers, how particular spaces will work for them, and to paint an appealing picture of moving day.

Do not show homes to your prospect which have already been sold to someone else if they are obviously superior to your current selection. This can do irreparable damage to your later efforts to create urgency and fear of loss.

7. *Selling The Neighborhood*

As you bring your product to life, you have the opportunity to bring the neighborhood to life as well. The more time you have to do this, the better. It is ideal if you can walk to the lots you want to show. If you need to take a car, drive as slowly as possible.

Within the spirit of the Equal Housing Opportunity laws, tell your prospect as many specifics about their future neighbors as is appropriate.

Selling the community is a time to create a mood of happiness. Talking about "that one jerk in ten that nobody can ever please" will not increase your prospect's comfort level on the way to the lot as well as happy stories will. The better prepared you are with anecdotes of happy, fulfilled, charitable neighbors, the better positioned you will be to sell this factor in the home-buying decision which, to many buyers, is the most important one of all.

Tell anecdotes about buyers in particular homes which you can point to. You especially want to tell experiences to which your prospects can relate in terms of their own needs and interests. Work in your third-party endorsements whenever possible. What was it which so many other people found here that made them choose this community out of all the other alternatives?

When possible, tell about buyers who bought the same model, or who live on lots which are similar to those you are showing. You are using the visit to the lot to increase your prospect's comfort level with your home, the community, your builder and yourself.

Throughout the lot-showing tour, it is important once again not to slip into monologue. Make sure your prospects get equal time. They need to express themselves, and you need the feedback. One of the very damaging things you can do in a sale is to establish momentum and then to start down a wrong avenue without even knowing it. The farther you proceed down that wrong avenue, the more you hurt your chances of making the sale. This is why it is so important to be continuously soliciting feedback, even if the feedback is negative.

8. Choosing A Favorite Lot

In showing lots you take maximum advantage of real estate's primary aspect: every piece of real estate is unique. If your customers are willing to buy your product, then there is one individual home/lot combination which is better for them than all the others. Your goal in showing lots is to reach agreement with your customers as to which lot is the best one for them. Not the ideal one, or the perfect one, but rather the best for them. This is a critical distinction. As we discussed in the chapter on "Overcoming Objections," do not feel ashamed, apologetic or discouraged that you are selling in an imperfect world. Your goal is to show your customers that the package which you are offering is better for them than the other real, available alternatives, and better for them than where they are living now: better for their lifestyle needs, and better from an investment standpoint.

If your transaction has gotten this far, chances are you already have both credibility and momentum on your side. The one piece which completes the selling puzzle is urgency. Naturally, urgency is easy to create if your project is nearly sold out, or if your prospect truly believes that your prices will increase substantially. But suppose you are in the early stages of the community, and your market is slow enough that prices are not increasing at the moment.

In showing lots, you set the stage for creating urgency by getting the customer to agree that:
1. there is one lot available today which is uniquely better suited to him than all of the others which you have available today, and
2. the future is uncertain.

While waiting for a future section is often an option, this

course of action is one which most people regret. Just as most homebuyers who procrastinate in making their decision wind up regretting the fact that they waited, those buyers who act decisively are usually glad they did. Many buyers wind up purchasing homes which would be out of their price range a year later. (For most people in this country, their home purchase is the most profitable investment they ever make.)

One of the ways of preparing for the lot-showing stage of SAM is to pick the lot which you would buy yourself, or would recommend to a close friend. (At this point I will use the term "lot" to refer to a particular combination of lot, model and elevation.) Then prepare the strongest possible a case for this lot. If there are several candidates for "best lot," then go ahead and prepare a case for each of them. If the homes are presited, then choose the best lot for each model type. Of course, you should be able to point out unique benefits of every one of your lots, but I believe it is good to have one or two which you feel particularly strong about.

I believe that in selling homes you should take your best shot first. I have heard others contend that you should save your best for last. I disagree because I believe that the single most powerful weapon in your selling arsenal is momentum. Any strategy which jeopardizes that momentum is extremely risky, and should be avoided whenever possible.

How do you take your weak shot first anyway? Do you fake enthusiasm for it, and then try to display that same enthusiasm for your second and third offerings? Or do you admit up front that you are saving the best for last and risk letting the buyer believe that you are toying with him?

To convey your strongest enthusiasm and conviction, and to do the most powerful job of emotional selling, **sell the way you would sell to a close friend:** you have gotten to know the prospect and his needs, and you are trying to get him the home which is the best value for the money, and the best home for his lifestyle.

Since no one can know the buyer as well as he knows himself, you must realize that your first choice for him may not be the same as his first choice for himself. So you pick the one you believe he will like the best, and you explain why you think it's the best. Then you show a few other possibilities just to be sure he can make the most informed decision possible.

I believe in a straight-shooting approach to showing lots. You will always do what you think is right with the most enthusiasm and the strongest conviction. Also you minimize the risk of losing your momentum by showing the prospect a turkey just as he is in the process of getting emotionally involved.

If the prospect disagrees with your first choice, do not go on a stubborn crusade to defend your position. Let the prospect make the ultimate decision as to his own first choice, and then get him to articulate his decision so that you can understand it. You may need to reinforce it later during your close.

Naturally, your prospect may raise objections to even your best lot. Hopefully the principles discussed in Chapter Three will help you overcome these objections.

9. Creating Fear Of Loss

After you have shown your prospect the lots and he has picked his favorite, get him to pick his second favorite as well. By doing this you will be creating urgency and fear of loss. Your objective in narrowing the prospect down to one lot is partly to enhance the value of that particular lot. For the same amount of money, the prospect can buy either his first or second favorite. The favorite obviously has more value, so there is more urgency to buy it. If your prospect likes one particular lot best, it is reasonable to assume that the next customer who walks in will like it best, too. The thought which you must plant in your prospect's mind is, "What if someone else gets it, after you saw it first, just because they were more decisive? You will then be stuck spending the same amount of money and getting only your second favorite, while someone else got the home that should have been yours."

Again urgency has been created, and a fear of loss which includes jealousy — the fear that someone else will benefit from their misfortune, and get the home they most wanted.

The important objective is to begin to set up the close by getting your prospects to narrow their focus to one "favorite," "unique" property — that property which is the best value and the best home for them — and to use this decision to begin the closing process.

10. The Home Stretch—Beginning Your Close

As the buyer narrows his focus and begins to form an emotional attachment — a preliminary sense of ownership — to one particular home and homesite, urgency is increasing and momentum is accelerating.

Do not lose sight of the fact that your potential competition can come from three sources:

a. Other available new homes.

Here your mission is to show that you meet more of the prospect's needs, and can offer a better value and lifestyle, than other available new home alternatives.

b. Resales

You must achieve the same recognition of superiority as in your new home competition, and also establish the superior benefits of function, quality, style and investment value which new homes have over "used" homes.

c. The prospect's current home.

This is often your fiercest competitor. You must not allow your prospects to slip back into complacency once they have expressed the desire to move. You are a doctor whose job is to locate the pain which caused the prospect to seek a doctor in the first place. You must then prescribe the appropriate cure. Sometimes the patient decides to avoid the cure and go on living with the pain. The doctor's job is to remind the patient that if pain goes untreated, it is likely to get worse. The doctor may even have to poke at the painful spot to remind the patient of the importance of taking constructive action.

Like the doctor, the new home salesperson devotes his or her career to relieving pain — "quality-of-life pain." You must sell the patient on the fact that your treatment is better than his pain, and that his pain will only grow more difficult and costly to cure as time goes on. In buying a new home, as in curing an ailment, procrastination can often make the solution much more difficult to achieve.

In medicine, this process is called treatment.

In new home sales, it is called closing.

Summary

Showing lots is the climax of the selling process. Emotional selling, creating visions, generating urgency and fulfilling needs all reach their peak of momentum at this stage. If you are successful in sustaining momentum through this stage, you frequently return to the sales office with a commitment to purchase already verbalized.

Keep focused on SAM with the "numbers game" in mind: get one out of every five prospects to the lot, and then close one out of three. This is how you can get a one in fifteen closing ratio.

It is important to understand ten critical dynamics of showing lots, and then to devise strategies for maximizing the opportunities which these dynamics present:

1. Emotional selling
2. Creative selling
3. Bringing the transaction to life
4. Controlling the selling environment
5. Increasing customer involvement
6. Enhancing your credibility
7. Selling the neighborhood
8. Choosing a favorite lot
9. Creating fear of loss
10. Beginning the close

These ten dynamics provide the key to increasing your momentum in the selling transaction through the final stages of your **Strategy to Achieve Momentum** and achieving your ultimate goal — the completed sale.

Action Items

1. For each unit type which you currently have on the market, pick the lot which you believe will be the next to sell and tell why. Using this information, develop a strategy for creating urgency for your next prospect to buy each lot which you have selected.
2. Prepare positive, relevant information about as many neighbors as possible. This will help you to sell the neighborhood and to employ third-party endorsements as you show lots.
3. List potential advantages or objections for each of the lots which you currently have on the market. Prepare how you will demonstrate the advantages and overcome the objections.
4. Make a list of construction features and benefits to demonstrate in the homes already under construction which you are unable to demonstrate in completed models.

CHAPTER SEVEN

Closing

Closing is the culmination of everything you have been focused toward from the beginning of your **Strategy to Achieve Momentum.**

In your first ten minutes you established rapport with your customers and began to learn their individual needs and motivations: "What is it about their present home which is causing them pain?" And, "How can you provide the cure in order to make the sale?" In the first ten minutes you have also presented your concept as the foundation for your total package, and you have presented your product's "unique selling premise."

Throughout the transaction you have sought to increase the customer's comfort level with you, your company, your community and your product.

You have learned the customers' needs, and then you have attempted to fulfill those needs. You have even exposed needs which your customers did not realize they had. As you have shown the interest and ability to fulfill those needs, you have gradually gained control of the selling environment.

You have demonstrated sales office displays, model homes and lots within the context of fulfilling your customers' needs, thereby maintaining control of the selling environment, strengthening your relationship with your customers, and sustaining selling momentum.

You have overcome objections by taking these objections out

of the context of the customers' ideal world and putting them into the context of the other real alternatives. You have kept the focus on your product as a total package, the integrated whole of which is greater than the sum of its separate parts.

While your approach has been primarily an emotional sell, you have continued to reinforce value at each stage of SAM. Finally you have narrowed your customers' focus down to one particular house type and lot—"the best one available."

In order to execute that final step—closing—you must meet one final challenge. And this is sometimes the greatest challenge of all—creating urgency.

Closing is where three primary elements of your strategy all come together in the "grand finale:"

1. Increasing comfort level.
2. Fulfilling needs.
3. Creating urgency.

These three pieces make up the puzzle we call selling. When all three of these pieces fit together, the stage is set for the close. A close which is attempted before these pieces are together may be useful from the standpoint of getting customers to articulate their present position, but it is unlikely to result in a sale except in the easiest of markets.

One aggressive school of sales thought says that you begin closing shortly after you begin establishing rapport with your prospect, and then continue to close periodically until you are successful. For those of you who are successful with this method, I will say nothing to discourage you. But for most salespeople this approach cannot work. It is the antithesis of the **Strategy to Achieve Momentum**, and threatens to undermine the very momentum which it seeks to achieve. SAM revolves around the principle of creating involvement by increasing the customer's comfort level and fulfilling needs. Closing too quickly is very threatening to many customers, and shows a disregard for individualism and need fulfillment. Fast closing is a valid approach for easy-to-sell jobs where sales are made at a faster rate than the homes can be delivered. This approach "knocks out" those prospects who are less decisive and possibly less qualified, and plucks only the "cream of the crop" from the superabundance of buyers for your product. If you are in a situation like that, go ahead with the fast close as long as it works for you.

In a normal selling environment, however, it is well worth the effort of planning and structuring your selling strategy so that the critical three pieces of the puzzle are in place as you begin your close.

If you've done the best you can with your strategy and sequence, and you're still not sure if the pieces are in place, going for the close may be the best way to find out. However, if you have successfully progressed through the first seven stages of SAM, then it is time to go for the close no matter what. At that point there's nothing to lose and everything to gain.

When you keep focused on SAM, you may not be closing the prospect from the minute he walks in the door, but you are incorporating a closing mindset from the beginning. This is ultimately a much more effective closing approach.

I have discussed the first two pieces of the selling puzzle increasing comfort level and fulfilling needs. Now I will focus more closely on the final piece—creating urgency.

Creating Urgency

I began to discuss creating urgency in the last chapter on "Showing Lots." Some of the points discussed require a second look now, since they also relate to your closing strategy.

There are several ways of creating urgency. The easiest situation is when an urgency factor is built into your circumstances.

"Prices are going up next week [or in the next section]."

"This is the last one of your model which backs up to the woods."

"The next section is less desirable."

"This is the last [only] home of your type that we have in your time frame."

More often, you have to create your own urgency. As discussed in the last chapter, in the real estate business you have an advantage which people who sell other products do not have: the fact that every piece of real estate is unique. Just as you must know the unique selling premise of your product and project, you must also prepare a unique selling premise for each home/lot combination (or unit, if it's a condominium) which you are trying to sell.

If you are selling single family homes, there are a number of possibilities to consider:
- Does a particular lot have the largest front or back yard?
- Does it have the flattest yard?
- Does it have the best view out of the front or back?
- Does it have the largest distance to the next home on the side or in the back?
- Does it have a particular sun exposure which may make it more appealing to most buyers?
- What about the next door neighbors, or the ones across the street? Are the kids the same age? Or babysitting age? Do the adults have anything in common which could make them ideal neighbors?

Neighbors can sometimes be even more important if you are selling townhomes or condominiums, as can such factors as view or sun exposure.

If you are selling townhomes:
- Do some of the units back directly up to other townhomes while others do not?
- How many homes have both the floorplan and the elevation which the prospect prefers?

If you are selling condominiums:
- What level is the unit on?
- How close is the parking?
- How close are the amenities?

All of these questions can provide motivators.

The point is not to be discouraged if your homes don't back up to trees. Most homes don't. No matter what your selection is, there's always one of that selection which is best for your buyer.

What about the home which has been completed for four months and has not sold because it really is on the worst lot? Naturally, if it is that bad, the pricing strategy should provide an incentive to the buyer who can move quickly or who is less affected by the objection. Instead of focusing on the lot, you might choose another unique selling premise: perhaps the exterior, or the neighbors, or the landscaping possibilities of the larger front yard which caused you to have a smaller back yard. You might simply emphasize the fact that the home is completed, and therefore less risky. Inventory homes offer the more cautious buyer with the best of both worlds. They get to see their home in every detail before they commit to it, which normally they only get if they buy a resale. They also get the superior features, quality, investment potential and warranty of a new home, and they are more likely to know who the neighbors will be.

When we discussed urgency in the last chapter, we provided a backup plan for those prospects who are able to pick out their favorite lot, but who want to wait to make a commitment. Create a fear of loss by having them pick out a second favorite lot along with their favorite. They should do this because if they like a particular lot better than all the others, chances are the next person who walks in the door will also like the same lot. If the next person is quicker, he might get that lot first, even though he was the last to see it. We have all seen this happen, causing heartbreak and embarrassment for people who did not act when they made their buying decision. Sometimes you need to tell these stories about the misfortunes of others to your prospect. It can be more of a service than a pressure tactic.

Fear of loss is a powerful motivator, especially when combined with the emotion of jealousy. Not only will the prospect fail to get the home he wants, but someone else will get it instead. Many people wind up making the decision to get married from just this type of stimulus. Being terrified of the commitment of marriage, they finally become motivated to take the step. It's not simply the fear of losing the loved one that changes their mind. It's often the jealousy of losing that loved one to ***someone else***.

Jealousy can be an extremely powerful closing tool for any product which is unique, and especially for homes. No one wants the biggest investment of his or her life to be the "leftover," while someone else got the best one.

Tell anecdotes of other people who have hesitated and lost, including yourself. The fact is that in the real estate business people who make the decision to buy are almost always glad they did, while people who decide to wait usually regret it. This truth can be reinforced with first and third-party endorsements. While would-be buyers are waiting for their ideal home to come along, the "real-life" selections in good locations and affordable price ranges continue to dwindle. Housing does not typically get easier to buy as time passes.

Creating urgency through the messages of the last few pages is not a hard-sell, strong-arm tirade. It's telling it like it is, kindly and caringly. How you express this message—how long you talk and what words you use—will, of course, depend upon your clientele. Whoever your market is, be careful not to talk down to them. You are talking to them now as a friend, not as a pedagogue. You're trying to help them balance their thoughts. You're not on a crusade to protect them from themselves. You are encouraging them, not flogging them. You're allowing them to benefit from your experience, the experience of other experts, and the experience of your previous customers.

One final point on creating urgency: get your prospects involved with as many specifics as possible. Not only the model, lot and elevation, but options, colors, anything which will deepen their attachment to your product. This sort of involvement generally begins with the model demonstration, continues through the lot selection, and re-emerges where necessary at the close.

The Closing Moment

Is there really a closing moment?

There is so much more to the close than merely a single decisive statement or action. In one sense, everything up to this point has been about closing. The whole purpose and focus of the **Strategy to Achieve Momentum** is closing. SAM is ultimately designed to create an environment in which the close is emotionally comfortable for both you and your prospect. Your

Closing

goal all along has been to increase the buyer's comfort level, and this objective must not come unraveled at the closing moment.

Whether or not there is a "closing moment," there absolutely must be a specific moment at which you clearly and decisively ask for the order. So for our purposes here I will call that the "closing moment."

The closing moment is, and should be, individualistic. There is no one-and-only, proper way to close. Experimenting with different styles, techniques and "lines" is well worth the risk. Occasionally a technique that you don't think has a chance will turn out to be more effective than your current method. However, if after several attempts you don't become comfortable with a particular closing technique, then drop it and try a different one.

The important thing is to make your closing style consistent with the rest of your selling style. This keeps the moment of "asking for the order" from being awkward or surprising. As with a golf swing, you get more distance if it feels comfortable than if it feels powerful.

I have seen top new home salespeople from all over the country prove the incredible diversity of successful closing styles.

I have heard several superstars say that the most effective closing method for them is to simply sit down and begin writing when the customer is hot, and then keep writing until the customer stops them. Others feel more comfortable making their request for an order more humorous. Some use the line, "Is there any reason not to go ahead and sign an agreement today?" They believe that this approach will either succeed immediately or, if it fails the first time, will at least get the objections out on the table where they can be dealt with immediately.

Some salespeople whose selling styles are especially natural and comfortable find it easy to ask for the order at the particular homesite which the buyer has chosen by simply saying, "Would you like to have this home?"

I like this approach for several reasons:
1. It results from and builds upon the high comfort level which the salesperson has achieved by developing personal rapport, building value, and narrowing the prospect's focus.

It is totally natural.
2. It is decisive and demands a decisive response, yet it is non-threatening. I even like the use of the word "have," instead of "buy" or "own," which do not connote the same warmth.
3. It is very simple and straightforward, which demonstrates confidence. There is no reason to make your request for the order cagey if you have established rapport and gained the customer's trust. You know why your customers are there, and they know why you're there. Why spoil it with gimmicks?

In my own selling, I designed the close to be the natural result of an approach which, from beginning to end, focused primarily on a combination of expertise, confidence and personal caring. I would begin closing during the lot-showing process by "testing the water:" explaining my builder's procedure for allowing a home to be taken off the market. This preliminary explanation of the closing process prior to the actual "closing moment" would serve two purposes:

1. Bringing up the issue of closing before the time came to ask for the order made the "closing moment" more familiar and comfortable for my customers when it finally happened.
2. It allowed me to evaluate customers' responses to receiving this information. If they offered immediate resistance, I could make the necessary adjustments before the "closing moment."

I always tried to ask for the order on the homesite. The approach was soft sell, but conveyed a quiet confidence and left the buyer with warm, comfortable feelings about the product, the community, the builder and me. Once a particular lot had been chosen, the "closing moment" would vary with the product, the market, and sometimes even with the individual customer. My most aggressive approach ("benevolent aggressiveness") was to ask the closing question with complete frankness. Speaking frankly and using normal words that the buyer expects to hear (like "contract" and "money") are not threatening at this point, but are natural and help to demonstrate your own confidence.

"Would you like to have this home?"

"Yes, I think this is the one we want."

"OK, then, if you're ready to take it we can go back to the sales office and I'll write up a contract for you."

At the opposite end of my spectrum of closing approaches was extreme soft-sell. The following approach is certainly not appropriate for every situation, or even for every salesperson. However, I found it very effective for closing customers who really wanted to buy, but were not willing to make the ultimate commitment that day. If the chances seemed better than 50/50 that the customer would buy within a week, and if I felt that I could afford to tie the home up for several days, then this approach would keep me from losing the customer to someone else on the day when they "became ready to buy."

I would explain to the buyer that my builder did not require customers to buy a home on the same day that they made their initial buying decision. "We encourage our customers to take several days to make sure they are positive before signing the actual contract. Until that time their deposit is refundable. That way we can be sure to have a community of homeowners who are happy with their buying decision. This helps to create a better neighborhood, and also more referral business for us."

I would offer this explanation in order to position my company as compassionate, responsible and wise, and to show that we were dealing from a position of strength: we did not want to lose a buyer, but we were not afraid to lose one.

Having established this position, I would close for the order by simply asking, "Would you like to go ahead and take the home off the market?"

While I would occasionally have buyers who would not go through with their contracts after putting down a refundable deposit, I believe I gained far more net sales than I would have with any other strategy, considering my personality and overall selling method.

Whatever closing method you can execute most comfortably and effectively, make sure you focus your whole **Strategy to Achieve Momentum** toward that close, and not let it drop when you get there. Selling is still fundamentally a numbers game. The farther you get through the sequence with a prospect, the more your chances of achieving a sale increase. By the time you get your prospect to focus on a particular lot, your chances of making a sale can be as high as one in three. This makes it well worth your while to get every prospect as far through SAM as they will allow.

Finally, know when to stop selling. Too often a sale is killed because the salesperson keeps talking after the customer has already decided to buy, and the salesperson unwittingly sets a new trap for himself.

Summary

Closing prematurely can do more harm than good, unless you are on a project which has achieved such momentum that fast closing is necessary to keep you from wasting time on unviable prospects. On an average or slow-paced project, closing occurs once rapport has been established, needs have been identified and a home has been selected. A premature close can be unnecessarily threatening, and is a dangerous tactic in a competitive market where the prospect has plenty of options. Opening greetings such as, "Nice day to buy a new home, isn't it?" don't cut it in the real world. Stick to your **Strategy to Achieve Momentum**, and the appropriate time to ask for the order will become apparent.

In order for the selling momentum to progress into a close, the customer must feel a sense of urgency. The best source of urgency is real circumstances: a hot market, a limited supply, rising prices or a particular circumstance in the customer's situation (such as needing to move within 30 days). If you are fortunate enough to have such circumstances, use every opportunity to create and reinforce the urgency.

If you do not have obvious urgency motivators, you must take your best shot from what you do have. Whatever your current selection of homes may be, there is always one which is best for each individual buyer. Once you have selected that best available home, use its unique advantages to create urgency. Then create fear of loss, and jealousy of someone else winning out at your prospect's expense.

On one level, "closing" may be defined as the moment when you ask for the order. On another level, closing is a mentality which begins when you first meet the customer, and is the ultimate object of your entire **Strategy to Achieve Momentum**. Along the way there are "mini-closes" as you attempt to gain feedback from the prospect's responses. Mini-closes also occur as you get the customer involved with specific elements or options which require secondary decisions.

When you do finally ask for the order, be sure your closing style is consistent with the personal selling style which you have used throughout the transaction. Whatever style you use, "asking for the order" must be a clearly defined action to which the prospect must respond with a decision. Don't count on telepathy, body language or subtle hints to convince the buyer to make a commitment. While some buyers will actually take the intiative to initiate the contract, they are the exception.

This chapter proposed several alternatives for executing "the closing moment." There are many more. You can make your "closing moment" uniquely your own.

Action Items

1. Make a list of all the tools you have which can help to create urgency for the homes you currently have on the market. (If there are items you do not have, but which you believe could help you to create urgency, you might want to suggest these strategies to your builder.)
2. Imagine that you are out on the site completing the process of showing lots. Your prospect has selected a favorite house type and lot, and you are now preparing to return to the sales office.
    a. How would you choose your closing moment?
    b. How would you ask for the order?

Envision as many scenarios as you think would be relevant.

CHAPTER EIGHT

Follow Up

What do you do about the prospects who express interest in your homes but do not reach the closing stage? Follow up is the key. The effectiveness of follow up has been debated for as long as the business of selling new homes has existed. My experience in talking with many salespeople, successful and unsuccessful, has shown a distinct and undeniable pattern. Those who persevere in a follow up program with a diligent, long-term commitment claim that it works. Those who don't persevere claim that it doesn't.

The idea of follow up gets more resistance from new homes salespeople than any other part of the selling process. The two main arguments against follow up are:

1. It yields minimal results.
2. It offends the prospect.

Many new home salespeople are intimidated by follow up. This could be partly because, unlike salespeople in general brokerage, new home salespeople are accustomed to having the entire transaction occur on "their turf." In follow up they lose that home court advantage. Follow up occurs on neutral territory—the telephone.

Two things, then, can seem more intimidating about follow up than selling on site:

1. You feel that you are invading the customer's privacy on their turf.

2. You have less control over the interaction (or selling environment) over the telephone than you do on the job site.

What is the mentality of the successful salesperson who can follow up confidently and productively? Those salespeople who are most successful at it do not view follow up as an invasion of privacy, but rather as part of the total service which they are offering. This is the same mentality discussed for effective model demonstration.

The superstars realize that most prospects have one basic trait which nearly all people share: we want attention. Attention is gratifying. It makes us feel important. It is only when the attention we get seems purely selfish or manipulative that we become annoyed. We especially deserve unselfish, caring attention when we are making the biggest purchase of our lives.

Top salespeople realize that if the attention they give the prospect in the form of followup is more service-oriented than self-oriented, the prospect will usually like the attention more than they dislike it.

The prospect realizes that the salesperson is getting a substantial commission, and he wants the salesperson to earn that commission just as the prospect has to earn his income at his job. Even customers who know very little about sales realize that follow up is part of a diligent salesperson's obligation, and they expect it as a natural course of events. They expect it and they respect it, as long as it is not obnoxious.

As with model demonstration, salespeople who view follow up as a service rather than as a sales technique feel much more comfortable pursuing it.

Although follow up is the one part of the transaction which does not occur on your "geographic" territory, you can still keep it in your "psychological" territory. As discussed earlier, you can maintain control of the selling environment as long as you can continue to fulfill the prospect's real needs. Although you rarely have as much control over the environment by phone as you have in person, you can still increase the control you do have by focusing on the buyer's needs. Therefore, do not follow up just for the sake of following up. Do it for the sake of providing a service. As with any other aspect of the sales presentation, the better prepared you are, the more effective you will be.

Since maintaining your prospect's comfort level is another part of your objective, it often helps if the prospect is also prepared for your follow up. One way to prepare your prospects for a follow up call is simply to ask their permission: "Do you mind if I give you a call sometime to see how your search is progressing?" It's even better if you can establish a specific reason for the call: "As soon as I get that piece of information for you, I'll give you a call." If you have succeeded in establishing a non-threatening image and good rapport with your customers, they will rarely deny you a follow up effort. If they do, then the follow up call probably could not have been productive with them anyway, and you may as well know it in advance. There is still no harm done.

Whenever possible, have a significant piece of information to give them during the follow up, whether they were expecting information from your call or not. "When you were out last weekend, you were wondering what the driving time would be from here to your work. I wanted to be able to give you a real answer and not just a guess, so I went out and drove it myself this morning. It took me exactly 26 minutes."

Another example would be, "You were asking if backing up to the high wire would pose any potential health risks. I found an article on the subject which I thought might interest you."

If you are making an unsolicited follow up phone call, sometimes a handwritten note to the prospect prior to the call will help pave the way.

Keep notes on personal items about the prospect to use as icebreakers when you call. Personalization is as important in follow up as it is in any other phase of the selling transaction.

If you publish periodic company newsletters, be sure to use them as additional follow up tools with your buyers.

How well does a good follow up program work? Top salespeople who make a consistent commitment to follow up claim that it increases their sales by 10% to 30%. Their follow up is successful not just because they make the calls, or even because they

convey additional valuable information, but because their program has tangible sales objectives:
1. To keep themselves in the forefront of the prospect's mind after the prospect has seen a number of competitors.
2. To give prospects the assurance that they are truly important in the salesperson's eyes.
3. To get additional feedback from prospects as to whether there are any other steps which the salesperson can take to sell them a home.
4. To generate another visit by your prospect to the community.

There is another reason why salespeople who persevere in follow up frequently outsell their competition. Follow up is part of a larger mentality of working harder in order to generate more of your own sales. Salespeople who are more committed to their follow up programs are typically salespeople who work harder in general. So they often have a total program which generates more sales than their competitors by virtue of their own personal diligence. In addition to following up, these salespeople are typically more diligent in three other areas:
1. Making sure their presentation is always first-rate.
   a. Freshness and cleanliness of model homes.
   b. Seasonal touches in models.
   c. Making the models look, feel and even smell homey.
   d. Complete, fresh on-site and off-site signage.
   e. A neat, well-organized sales office.
   f. Clean, well-maintained inventory homes.
2. Demonstrating models and showing lots more regularly, thoroughly and energetically than their competitors.
3. Prospecting—attempting to generate a significant percentage of their traffic by themselves. Top salespeople realize the potential for generating customers which lies beyond the boundaries of their builder's advertising budget. Prospecting involves pioneering into the marketing frontier, and for many requires more initiative than any other aspect of new home sales. As with follow up, salespeople who make a long-term commitment to prospecting testify

to its value as a source of additional sales. The percentage can vary with the product, location and conditions, but generating one-third of your traffic and sales through prospecting is a realistic goal for those who commit to a complete program. The most widely-accepted methods of prospecting are:

a. Calls, visits and flyers to real estate offices.
b. Visiting employment centers.
c. Getting referrals during the follow up process.
d. Asking prospects who don't buy for referrals.
e. Generating referrals from previous buyers by telephone, mail, personal visits and community parties to which homeowners may invite prospective buyers as guests.
f. Building a referral-generating mechanism into your customer service program. Customers who are treated attentively after their contract is signed, and who are happy with the quality of construction and service, are naturally your best, and least expensive, source of sales.

One final thought on follow up is this: Feedback is a fringe benefit of follow up even when you have had a period of poor sales results. Salespeople who remain committed to follow up through hot streaks and cold streaks feel as though they have more control of their total situation. When prospects are not buying, these salespeople know why; and they find out where, if anywhere, their prospects finally do buy. If they are not buying anywhere, that is a much different problem than if they are buying primarily from one or two new home competitors. It means something else if they are buying mostly in the surrounding resale market, or in more remote and less expensive locations. In any of these cases, the salesperson is able to provide answers and suggest remedial steps. Sometimes feedback merely gives you the peace of mind to know that you and your builder are doing everything right, and must simply lower your expectations for a period of time. Even that is better than beating your head against a wall in bewilderment.

Summary

Unlike the eight stages of SAM, follow up is mostly discipline and attitude. While creativity and technique may appear to play a smaller role in follow up than in the subjects of previous chapters, that in no way detracts from its importance. The same **Successful Sales Mentality** discussed throughout this book is what produces successful follow up.

Follow up is important as a vehicle for:
1. Keeping yourself in the forefront of the prospect's mind.
2. Showing your prospects that they are important to you.
3. Getting feedback and updating your prospect's status.
4. Generating another visit by your prospect to your community.

Successful salespeople increase the effectiveness of their follow up by viewing it as a service more than as a selling technique. They personalize their follow up whenever possible, and try to increase the value of the follow up to the prospect by conveying new information. They also look for opportunities to lay the groundwork for a follow up opportunity during the prospect's visit to the community.

Even when the follow up fails to generate a sale, the feedback you gain can help you create effective sales and marketing strategies for the future.

Action Items

1. Plan several ways of getting your prospects' permission to follow up with them before they leave your project.
2. As you write out your comments on each of your prospect registration cards, conclude with a strategy for following up with them. Include a piece of personal information about them to help you re-establish rapport during your call.

CHAPTER NINE

Difficult Situations

At this point I have finished dealing with the execution of specific stages of the selling process. The last two chapters will address a variety of situations for which it it is important to be prepared, even though they are not necessarily part of the salesperson's daily experience. If you can anticipate and prepare for these difficult circumstances, you will find them less stressful when they arise. In this chapter I will deal with five situations in particular:
1. Selling "preview openings."
2. Dealing with buyer's remorse.
3. Dealing with the irate purchaser who storms in when you're trying to sell a home to someone else.
4. Dealing with the antagonistic customer.
5. Dealing with the compulsive worrier.

Selling Preview Openings

There are valid arguments for and against "preview openings" — opening the project for sales before the models are completed.

The primary arguments in favor of waiting until models are completed are:
1. You can sell your homes for more money when you have finished models to show, so why give away that extra profit

on a preview opening?
2. You can create urgency by generating a waiting list and have a more successful grand opening when your models are completed.
3. You do not have to worry as much about misrepresentation if you are selling from finished models. Without models you increase your risk of creating ill will in two ways:
   a. Creating a wrong impression of your product.
   b. Making changes to your product during construction of the models.

The most important arguments which favor a preview opening are:
1. You can generate better cash flow by delivering your first homes earlier.
2. You can sell credibility and value at your grand opening by having homes already sold prior to completion of your models.
3. You can "learn" how to sell your product and create a smoother, more effective presentation by the time your models open.
4. You can determine any flaws in the product and correct them prior to model completion.

In order to create an incentive for people to buy during a preview, your builder must usually be willing to accept a lower price (by as much as 3% to 5%) than he would get after the grand opening. The customer who buys during a preview opening is typically more investment-oriented than buyers who need to see a model or finished home under construction. Since preview buyers are willing to take more risk, your pricing program should be structured to reward them by assuring them that you will charge higher prices to later buyers. This motivational statement occurs in your first ten minutes. As you introduce your concept, you tell your prospect that you are having a preopening in order to establish your momentum and credibility more quickly. To accomplish this your builder is willing to share his profits with customers who invest without seeing the models. Your builder believes that by taking this approach he is providing a better investment opportunity for the preview buyer, and that the builder will also be making a wise investment decision by implementing this strategy. It is not a giveaway on the part of the builder (you don't want to make your builder look scared or stupid). It is a plan that works for everybody.

Your **Strategy to Achieve Momentum** works essentially the same in a preview opening as it would work at any other time. After your first ten minutes comes the stage where you begin demonstrating the models. The fact that you don't have models can work for you more than it works against you if you have your strategy in place. Your prospects actually need you more without models than they do with models, so you have a better opportunity to create rapport and personal involvement with them. The lines of communication are even more important to these customers, and you can use that to your advantage in learning as well as teaching.

Since your prospects cannot escape from you into the models, you now "walk through" your homes with them by means of your brochure or blueprints. This situation provides you with an excellent opportunity to generate feedback from your customers and zero in on their individual needs. During your "demonstration," however, it is extremely important that you make sure they undertand what you are explaining to them, and that you are cautious in your promises concerning items which may be subject to change.

If your models are partially completed, go ahead and use them as an opportunity to sell construction and to create your vision. Explain to your buyer, if necessary, that homes seem smaller in early stages of construction, and then appear to "grow" as construction progresses. Although your customers may not express it, they frequently feel disheartened by how small a home feels in the early stages of construction. You can overcome this by expressing excitement at the metamorphosis which transforms a home as it progresses.

Using your brochures and blueprints, your goal is still to narrow the buyer's focus down to one model, and then to show them the appropriate lots. From this point on, everything works the same as the strategies already discussed.

Most preview openings are conducted from a trailer. While your trailer should be comfortable, some builders cannot justify the expense of an elaborate trailer. If this is your builder's position, then sell this strategy as a benefit. Sell the spartan conditions of your trailer as part of the ground-floor, low-overhead spirit of the preview opening which allows you to pass on additional savings to your first buyers.

If you have prospects who are interested in your product, but absolutely refuse to buy before seeing finished models, be frank with them. Admit to them that preview openings are not for everyone. As you continue to reinforce the benefits of buying before models are completed, also try to set the stage for follow up with these prospects after model completion. If they don't buy during your preview opening, you don't want to lose them forever. You simply want to be sure they understand the pros and cons of their position. Make sure they realize that they will probably have to pay more when the models are completed. Then explain that you understand that to some people that "insurance" is worth an extra few dollars a month. Some people can visualize from two dimensional drawings more easily than others can. Rather than trying to push your good but frightened prospects too aggressively on the first day, simply admit, kindly and compassionately, these truths about the homebuying process. Then assure them that people who do take the preview opening step are handsomely rewarded. Use stories of other people who have benefitted from this strategy, especially if they are people who have bought from you in preview openings at other communities.

Buyer's Remorse

The best time to deal with buyer's remorse — the feeling of regret which makes buyers want to cancel their contract — is before it sets in.

Naturally, buyer's remorse has different implications depending upon whether or not the buyer has the right to void his commitment and receive his money back.

If the buyer is bound to his contract but wants to get out of it and still receive his money, his approach may be aggressive, obnoxious, and possibly include false accusations.

Understanding your buyers' stress is necessary for you to be able to deal with them patiently and caringly, yet firmly and confidently. It is also important that you not take buyer's remorse personally, even if your buyers try to make it personal. Homebuying brings out the worst in some people, and dealing with the worst they can dish out comes with your territory. It is important for you to convey to them that you care about them as much now as you did before they signed their contract. Their self-esteem is already in jeopardy with buyer's remorse. It is important that no blows to their self-esteem come from you, no matter how they may be treating you at the moment.

Let them know that buyer's remorse is a natural stage in the homebuying process, as it is with other major decisions. Think of how many people develop second thoughts at some point during their engagement to be married, but work through the phase to arrive at the altar dressed up and on time. The homebuying process is not so different. Explain to your customers that most people who buy homes do experience buyer's remorse at some point during their purchase. People who let this natural period of doubt overwhelm them wind up having the most regrets in the end. As you explain this basic truth of homebuying to them, retrieve the tools you used to make the sale in the first place:

1. Recall for your buyers how they thoughtfully developed the decision to take this step in order to improve their lives.
2. Review the needs which were unfulfilled in their current home and now will be met in their new one.
3. Recall your anecdotes and third-party endorsements to remind your buyers that their decision to buy truly was a wise one which produced a positive step for their future.
4. Suggest to them, if necessary, that they take another week

to reevaluate their situation. (This will also give you more time to strengthen your arguments if you need to.)
5. But most important, maintain your patience, composure, confidence, and your position of strength. Don't grovel. You have conducted yourself with dignity and from a position of strength all along. Keep your high ground now to reinforce your relationship with your buyer.

Still, no matter what you say or how well you say it, the fact is that dealing with buyer's remorse is one of the most difficult, and often seemingly hopeless situations you face in new home sales. The strongest approach you can take in dealing with buyer's remorse is to anticipate and address it before it happens, while the buyer is on the high of making their positive decision, and before you have to take a defensive position. Here the cliche is relevant that "the best defense is a good offense."

Address the issue of buyer's remorse frankly at that moment when the buyer's commitment seems the strongest. While this may seem like an unnecessarily bold approach, your buyers will appreciate it, and they will be much more likely to accept and remember your message if they hear it during a period of confidence and positive momentum. Explain the normality of buyer's remorse, relate it to other large decisions which are familiar to them, and assure them that it passes as naturally as it sets in.

Saving a sale when the buyer is entitled to get his money back is even harder. Whether the buyer is entitled to a refund or not, preparation for buyer's remorse at the time the purchase is made is your most effective strategy.

One moment which can produce an opportunity for addressing buyer's remorse is immediately after the customer has signed his contract, as you are thanking him.

"I appreciate your buying a home from us, and I want to continue to give you all the help I can. If you think of some more questions please call me, and if I don't know the answer I'll get it for you. I know that buying a new home is a very emotional experience, and most people go through ups and downs after they buy. It's normal, and people work through it, but sometimes they just like to call me up and talk. Please feel free to do that whenever you want. I know you'll love your new home here, and again I really appreciate having you as a customer."

Other potential opportunities for addressing buyer's remorse may occur immediately before your customers sign their contract, or after they have selected their favorite lot and don't want to lose it. The important point here is that you set the stage for a position of strength concerning buyer's remorse at the time of the purchase. Then, if your customers come back after the contract wanting a refund, you already have a foundation to build on. Now you can take a patient but firm approach with them in which you:

1. Reawaken their discontent with their current situation.
2. Reassure them with:
   a) your product's strengths and benefits,
   b) their own previous reasoning, and
   c) third party endorsements.
3. Keep the atmosphere relaxed and don't be defensive.
4. Use the Ben Franklin pros and cons approach if you believe it would help.
5. Be sure you get them to tell their real problem so that you can stay on track by addressing the right issue.

The approach to buyer's remorse I am recommending here is intended for salespeople who believe they are having an abnormally high rate of kickouts due to buyer's remorse. As with other problem-solving suggestions which appear throughout this book, if you're not having the problem, then stick with your current, proven method.

All salespeople lose some sales to buyer's remorse no matter how good they are. In a country where the divorce rate is 50%, you can't expect to escape without any buyer's remorse kickouts. Don't take the occasional one personally. There are some you just can't help. Perhaps it was simply that you did your job so well in the first place that you succeeded in selling to someone you shouldn't have. How bad is that?

Dealing With The Irate Purchaser Who Storms In When You're Trying To Sell A Home To Someone Else

While this scenario is often the new home salesperson's worst nightmare, I have been amazed at how little damage it causes when it actually happens. Prospective purchasers seem to have the ability to take this type of incident in stride. Perhaps it's because they see this type of behavior so frequently, especially in the retail environment. They tend to think of it more as a reflection on the buyer than on the builder (unless it is a group of people at once, or an incident repeated by several people at different times).

Your best approach in this type of situation is to diffuse it by rising above it. Again it is important to deal from a position of strength. You can do this by introducing the irate buyer directly to your prospect, and perhaps even offering to discuss the buyer's problem in front of the prospect.

As you are discussing financing at your desk in the sales office with Mr. and Mrs. Albert, who are nearly ready to buy, Mr. Craig, who lives in one of your homes which is still under warranty, storms in and screams, "I've had it! My daughter's wedding reception is at our so-called home in six hours, she's getting married in four hours, the air conditioning doesn't work, and your subcontractor says it's not an emergency. Buying a home from you idiots is the worst mistake I ever made in my life!"

Your response, in a kind and even tone, is to welcome him into where you are talking with the Alberts, as opposed to sneaking into another room with Mr. Craig, where the Alberts will never know how you resolved Mr. Craig's problem.

"Come on in, Mr. Craig. I was just talking with Mr. and Mrs. Albert about financing..." (Then turn to the Alberts and continue)..."Mr. and Mrs. Albert, this is Mr. Craig. Would you mind sparing me a moment to help him? Contrary to what our subcontractor said, this really is an emergency..." (Then back to Mr. Craig.) "Mr. Craig, let me call the subcontractor myself right now and see if I can change his mind. If I can't, I'll find someone else who can come out today, and we'll take care of the finances later. In any event, the bill will not be your problem." You then make the appropriate calls, and tell Mr. Craig to call you back if his air conditioning is not working within a specified period of time.

Since this is an extreme example in which I have suggested a potentially controversial solution, it's a good idea to agree with your builder on a policy for handling such situations. Again, preparation can be your most valuable tool. In committing your builder (or possibly yourself, in the event that your builder does not support your action) to the financial resolution of this difficult situation, you have had to make a personal decision involving right and wrong, and also a business decision involving the Alberts as potential customers and the Craigs as potential referral sources. Had the problem been less severe, your goal would have been to promise a fair resolution as early as the problem could be addressed, and a prompt follow up call to your homeowner explaining the outcome.

The point is that you have used Mr. Craig as an additional opportunity to sell your company to the Alberts, while providing service to a valued customer. You have maintained your position of strength: you have shown that you are not intimidated by Mr. Craig's grandstanding by introducing him to the Alberts; and you have shown that you and your company are sincere, courteous and professional in dealing with your customers' problems.

Dealing With The Antagonistic Customer
Dealing With The Compulsive Worrier

While the antagonistic customer and the compulsive worrier may not produce exactly the same types of problems, I will discuss them together because I believe your mentality in dealing with them should be similar. Both of these problems are manifestations of buyer insecurity. A degree in psychology should not be a prerequisite to a career in new home sales, but understanding human nature is a tremendous asset, and can translate directly into a higher closing ratio and a lower kickout rate.

As with buyer's remorse, coping with the antagonistic customer or the compulsive worrier requires a patient and compassionate acceptance of basic frailty. Antagonism or worry could reach its peak at any of several points in the buying experience: prior to the contract, between contract and settlement, or even after settlement. The customer's behavior can become rude, annoying, or even unfair. It can sometimes make a salesperson more concerned with defending his rights and dignity than with going on about the business of making a sale, preserving a sale, or generating a referral. It is difficult to stay focused under these sorts of pressures. If you do your job honestly and competently your dignity requires no defense. Being a new home salesperson has been described as being the customer's "emotional punching bag," much like a doctor, lawyer, psychiatrist or accountant. A certain amount of abuse and annoyance simply come with the territory because you are dealing with people in a state of fear.

Who knows what causes customers to suddenly become aggressive or paranoid? Did someone "advise" them about the art of "winning through intimidation?" Did some friend brag to your buyers that he got a "better deal" than they did? Did parents second-guess your buyers' decision? Did your buyers receive less than they expected on their resale? Are they experiencing some personal adversity? Are they recoiling from some other mistake which they made in the past? Or are they simply timid, indecisive, or pessimistic people by nature? Since there are so many possibilities, and since you usually don't know the true answer, you must simply equip yourself with a mentality and a game plan which can deal with the antagonistic customer or the compulsive worrier.

Since one of the problems you are trying to deal with is your customers' insecurities, one of your goals is to bolster their self-esteem rather than threaten it. This can be particularly hard when your customers are on the attack. But if they are behaving like a threatened tiger, increasing the threat is not likely to calm them down. As with buyer's remorse, deal kindly but firmly. Don't threaten or criticize, but don't grovel either. Be sympathetic, but not submissive.

You may have a customer who stops into your sales office every weekend after walking through his home under construction and gives you a list of complaints.

"This is the third weekend we've seen that broken stud in the fourth bedroom upstairs. We mention it every week, and nothing's been done. Now there's water in the basement. If it's still there next weekend, we'll be talking to our lawyer about whether we should have our contract canceled."

A good response would be, "Mr. Matthews, you need to trust me on this. I haven't let you down yet, and I won't from this point on. The stud will be replaced before your home is drywalled. Typically a builder does repairs as late as possible because it's more efficient. They can fix more items at a time, make fewer trips back, and have your home ready to live in more quickly. As for the basement, it will often have some water before the windows are in and grading is completed. But then the wetness will stop, and it causes no damage in the meantime. I know it's tough to watch your own home being built. I don't think I could handle it as well as you have, because I know all the things that will go wrong before they're made right. But that's honestly the way the process works. Please don't second-guess yourself, because when we're done it really will be the way you want it."

While this response may seem a little long-winded, it demonstrates your knowledge, patience, respect for the customer, and the concern which your customer needs to see in order to be reassured.

With either the antagonistic customer or the compulsive worrier, sometimes just treating them well is enough to solve the problem. They'll be pleased to find that you are willing to listen.

As with buyer's remorse, you can head off some of the problems of insecurity in advance. You must be very careful with the level of expectations which you create within the prospect as you are trying to sell to them. Buyers pressure you to raise their expectations, and then lose respect for you when you do. Raising expectations beyond what you are sure you can deliver, or beyond what you need to make the sale, is risky business. This challenge becomes even greater when a market deteriorates, but the principle becomes no less important.

Top salespeople have convinced me again and again that they do accept the fact that extraordinary patience, sympathy and reassurance are part of their basic job description. Still, reality demands that you must set limits on how far you can go in hand-holding your more difficult customers. Your jobs are filled with a variety of responsibilities. Yet you still have sales quotas to make, and there are still only so many hours in a week. Once your customers demand more than you can afford to give them in the way of time or attention, there is nothing wrong with telling them that you have a job to do, just like they do, and that they must respect your other responsibilities. Sometimes you simply have no choice but to tell them, politely and respectfully, that if all your other customers demanded as much attention, your job would become impossible. One way you could say it is this:

"I will follow up on the items we discussed today, as I have in the past. But I need to ask a favor from you as well. I will certainly continue to honor every commitment that I have made to you, but I also have made these same commitments to twenty other people who have signed contracts but not yet settled. With all my other responsibilities, I need to ask that you simply trust me to make sure your items are handled in their proper sequence. I really do watch over all of my customers' homes, but that puts my time at a premium. I can only spend so much with each customer. You know how it is at your job."

Sometimes a customer will pester you to death, or even threaten the sale, between the time of the contract and the time of settlement. If you believe the customer is simply trying to test you, or to extract more from you, but not to get out of his contract, you might consider offering his money back. Just tell him, "I really can't do any more for you. If I can't satisfy you, I'd rather just give you your money back and sell your home to someone else who will benefit more from it."

This is, of course, an extreme step for extreme situations. Obviously your goal is not to give your buyers their money back, but rather to diffuse their aggressiveness by taking away what they consider to be their leverage — the fact that you need them more than they need you.

It also may help to defuse their fears that you could be trying to take advantage of them now that you have their deposit. By offering them their money back you are showing them that having their deposit does not change your attitude toward them. Giving them the best possible service always was and always will be your top priority, but fairness on both sides has to be part of the deal as well. Your goal is to preserve the sale, your integrity, and the customer's respect and good will.

Summary

This summary will highlight ways in which successful salespeople have dealt with the challenges discussed in this chapter. The nature of the material in this chapter and the next does not require the "Action Item" section which has followed the summary in each of the previous chapters.

I. *Preview Openings*
  A. Sell the value of buying at a preview opening by explaining frankly to your customer that the builder's strategy is to increase credibility and cash flow by "investing" in a discount to preview buyers.
  B. Use SAM the same way without models that would use it with models. Not having models often gives you a better opportunity to establish rapport with your prospects.
  C. Keep in touch with prospects who like what they hear at the preview opening, but who absolutely cannot buy without seeing finished models. Some customers really are willing to pay more for the same home in order to have the security of seeing a finished model, and of knowing that other buyers are already happily moved in. Treat these customers patiently and respectfully, and follow up with them when your models are completed.

II. *Buyer's Remorse*
  A. If you believe you are having an abnormally high kickout rate due to buyer's remorse:

1. Address the issue of buyer's remorse at the moment when your comfort level and your customers' are at their highest. This may be after they have selected their favorite lot and don't want to lose it; it may be as they are preparing to sign their contract; or it may be immediately after they have signed it.
2. Assure them that buyer's remorse is a natural part of the homebuying process, and that once buyers work through it, everything is fine. Buyers who are unable to work through it, succumbing to it instead, are usually the ones with regrets in the end.

B. When buyer's remorse does occur, deal with it patiently and caringly, but firmly. Encourage your customers to tell you, as candidly as possible, what their real concern is. Then reawaken their discontent with their current situation, and retrieve the enthusiasm which originally brought them to their buying decision.

III. *Dealing with Irate Purchasers in Front of Prospects*

A. This situation usually causes less damage than you expect it to, and often reflects worse on the irate purchaser than it does on you.

B. You can turn this situation to your benefit by addressing the issue kindly, respectfully and head-on in the presence of your prospect. You can even introduce the irate purchaser directly to the prospect to help demonstrate your honorable intentions and defuse the purchaser's assumed leverage.

IV-V. *Dealing with the Antagonistic Customer and the Compulsive Worrier*

A. Both of these types of customers require compassionate patience and respectful frankness. Dealing with customers who are experiencing unusual fear and stress comes with the territory of selling new homes. But there is nothing wrong with explaining to the buyer the many demands and responsibilities which you are obligated to meet, and that you must handle them all fairly and proportionately. Sometimes the bold strategy of offering a buyer his money back

is the only way of conveying a reasonable perspective to him — even if you intend the offer to be a "bluff."
B. The better you can make your customers feel about ***themselves***, the more favorably they are likely to view you, and their buying experience as a whole.

CHAPTER TEN

Slumps and Burnout

A **Successful Sales Mentality** is especially important when it comes to dealing with the unique set of stresses and emotional challenges associated with new home sales. You work weekends.

You spend extended periods of time in virtual isolation.

You earn your living trying to be accepted by customers who will reject you 95% of the time.

You are paid on commission, as though you have complete responsibility for your own productivity; and yet your income is determined largely by forces beyond your control, and does not always increase like the incomes of many of your friends in other lines of work.

Your efforts often go unappreciated by co-workers who see you at work only three days a week (and you arrive "late" on those days).

And, as discussed in the last chapter, you must fill the role of "emotional punching bag" for unappreciative customers.

All of this when you are at your best. So what happens when the market turns downward, or you slide into a slump?

I have talked frequently with top salespeople about what makes them cope better than so many of their colleagues. In this line of work, it is not unusual to see your peers get out of the business after several years, or during the first market downturn, or after failing to survive their own personal slump or burnout. I will try to pass on to you some of the thoughts which have helped superstars survive and prosper over the long haul in the face of their unique adversities.

I began the study of new home sales by talking about what it takes to succeed, and now have come full circle. After seeing how those characteristics help you to develop a **Successful Sales Mentality** it is time to look at how those same characteristics can help you to sustain your success in the face of the inevitable slumps and, for many, burnout.

Dealing With Slumps

Slumps happen to everyone, regardless of ability. While it is important to realize when you are in a slump, it is also important to realize that the slump is only as crippling as you allow it to be. Remember that while you may be in a slump, only you know it. The buyer walking in your door does not.

When you realize you're in a slump, try to incorporate the following thoughts into your **Successful Sales Mentality**.

1. Treat each new customer as a fresh opportunity. Whether or not the last ten prospects who walked into your door were ready, willing and able buyers does not affect the odds of whether the next prospect will be. It's like flipping a coin. The coin may come up tails ten times in a row, but the odds are still 50/50 that the next time it will come up heads. Don't superimpose past frustrations on your next prospect. Superimpose your past successes on him instead.

2. When recalling your past successes, also recall what you know to be your greatest selling strengths, and capitalize on them.

3. Remember that even in a market downturn, customers still buy primarily on emotion. Stimulate emotion through enthusiasm and action. Not only can your buyer catch it, but you may even catch it yourself.

4. Spend some of your spare time studying new sales techniques, especially books and tapes. Attend a few seminars if possible. You can discover tremendous revitalizing power in

these tools.
5. Spend your "down time" in the sales office preparing anecdotes and strategies for future use. Down time is ideal for doing the "Action Items" and other preparation work discussed throughout this book.
6. Shop competition more than ever. Many of your competitive colleagues can provide needed companionship. The knowledge you gain about the outside world can help put your own slump into perspective.
7. Remember that you are in a good business performing a valuable service.
8. Salespeople with a positive mental attitude and a sense of humor generally turn a slump around faster than others. There is truth to the cliche, "You're only in a slump as long as you think you're in a slump."
9. Maintain a long-term, big-picture mentality. While a market downturn may not be the best thing for your bank account, in the long run it actually can be one of the best things for your career. Those who began selling homes in a downturn generally look back on the experience as one of their greatest breaks. It teaches the profound truths of new home sales much faster, and much more permanently, than beginning in easier times.

Patience and long-term thinking can be very difficult for someone going through a downturn for the first time, but anyone who has been through one will tell you:
1. It does end.
2. You become a better salesperson for it.
3. It is ultimately a satisfying and gratifying experience for those who tough it out.
4. The good prospects and salespeople still succeed in a downturn.

Dealing With Burnount

Burnout has many of the same symptoms as slumps. In burnout, however, the helpless feeling you often sense in a slump

may be compounded by one or more of the following additional elements:
1. A feeling of emotional or physical exhaustion.
2. A feeling of extreme frustration, even outrage, with your product, your builder, your customers, or your total situation.
3. A sense of disoriention: "What am I doing here?" You may be questioning your whole career or sense of direction in life.

In preventing and combating burnout, the principles are largely the same as those for dealing with slumps.
1. Top salespeople say they are able to conquer burnout by keeping their total lives and priorities in balance through the burnout period.
2. Focus on maintaining a positive mental attitude, a sense of humor, and a long-term, big-picture mentality.
3. Concentrate on selling emotion and enthusiasm. Remember that your prospect does not know that you are suffering from burnout.
4. Stay focused on your **Strategy to Achieve Momentum**. SAM is one of your best friends for helping you to get through a slump, or to overcome burnout. SAM reminds you to keep planning that next stage, and not to self-destruct on your path toward the close. One of the ways slumps and burnout can be identified is that they cause you to subconsciously abort your mission as you approach the close. Your thought might be, "Don't waste the effort. You'll only be rejected anyway." It is critical that you ignore such thoughts, and view every prospect as a fresh opportunity to turn your slump around. Don't lose hope. Fight slumps and burnout with aggressive selling: "Only the customer can stop the transaction."
5. Prepare for burnout. If you can see burnout heading toward you in advance (and you often can), plan your job properly at the outset. Pace yourself to maximize your energy level during the hectic times, and use down times for vacation, relaxation or study. Like most other problems, burnout is

much easier to control if you start preparing for it before it arrives.
6. Burnout is a normal part of a new home sales career which, if handled properly, is only temporary. It is important not to panic, but to face it head on and work through it. As in working through slumps, remember above all that you really are in an outstanding profession, in which your own personal service and expertise improves people's lives. Not many people can say that.

Summary

Long-term success in new home sales requires an ability to sustain your focus throughout your mission. SAM is one mechanism which will help you to sustain this focus.

Long-term success also requires a long-term mentality. The ability to rise above the cycles and the stresses and to keep focused on a big-picture perspective will enable you to maximize both the easy situations and the more challenging ones. Salespeople with a **Successful Sales Mentality** gain more enjoyment, and stay on a more even keel, by developing good "emotional habits" which help them to sustain a healthy perspective. They accomplish this in several ways:

1. They continue to emphasize emotional selling.
2. They work hard at keeping their personal and professional lives in balance, and at pacing themselves properly through seasons and market cycles. They find ways to "recharge their batteries."
3. They maintain their sense of purpose by viewing their profession as a vital service, regardless of market conditions. Their positive mental attitude, sense of humor and friendships with their peers help them to sustain their self-image through slumps.
4. They recall their successes and stay focused on their strengths, and see each new customer as a fresh opportunity to relive their successes and exercise their strengths.

CHAPTER ELEVEN

Review

This book has been about developing a **Successful Sales Mentality** for selling new homes — a mentality which maintains a focus on momentum and closing throughout the various stages of the selling process. Developing this mentality makes the technical part of selling easier and more natural than sales strategies which rely on memorized questions, responses and behavior.

The basis for this mentality is a game plan which I have called the **Strategy to Achieve Momentum** (SAM). SAM is a series of eight critical stages (or goals), each of which is designed to propel you on to the next stage, and each of which is focused toward the ultimate close. SAM should not be confused with the normal chronological sequence of steps which occurs during the course of a sale (greeting, qualifying, demonstrating models, showing lots, explaining financing and closing), but it does not conflict with this sequence. In fact, SAM makes this more familiar sequence easier to accomplish. It keeps the selling process on track by focusing on the critical element of momentum. This momentum keeps the sale moving from one stage to the next, and continually increases the customer's involvement along the way. The **Strategy to Achieve Momentum** is reviewed below.

1. *Establish rapport with your customer.*
   A. Search for ways to establish "common ground" with your customer.

B. Your interaction with the customer must be a two-way conversation — an exchange of information. The conversation must never slip into lecture or monologue.

2. **Explain your concept to the customer.**
   A. The concept is "a concise statement of your product's unique significance."
   B. The concept is the foundation upon which your product presentation is built, and serves the additional purpose of distinguishing you from the rest of the market. With your concept you carve out your own unique territory in the mind of your customer.
   C. This stage of SAM occurs in "the first ten minutes," while you are creating rapport with your customer.

3. **Determine your customer's needs.**
   A. This process also begins during the first ten minutes and then continues through subsequent stages.
   B. It evolves from the rapport which you have developed.

4. **Show that your product fulfills the customer's needs.**
   A. Like all stages of SAM, this stage relies upon the success of the stage before, and helps build the urgency to continue to the next stage.
   B. Fulfilling needs is essential to winning the "battle" for control of the selling environment. As long as you are fulfilling needs, your customers believe that they have control of the selling environment, which makes them comfortable. But the fact is that you are controlling the selling environment because you are increasing your customers' involvement.
   C. Use third-party endorsements and anecdotes to help show your proven ability to fulfill your customers' needs. Use them also to create a more vivid vision for your customers of a life in which these needs are fulfilled.
   D. Make your customers realize additional needs which they have, but may not yet have focused upon.

5. **Lead the customer to pick out a favorite model.**
   A. This is accomplished, of course, at the conclusion of the model presentation.

B. During the model demonstration, focus on the home's features and benefits as they relate to the customer's individual needs, and not merely from a design standpoint.

6. *Lead the customer to pick out a favorite lot.*

A. This is SAM's most critical stage. Reaching this stage, and then capitalizing on it when you get there, is that part of SAM which will most increase your chances of making the sale.

B. It is during this stage that you are best able to:
  1. Sell the community (especially the neighbors who are the source of many of your third-party endorsements).
  2. Sell your builder's expertise, as well as your own.
  3. Begin the final stages of the close.

7. *Create in the customer's mind the fear of losing that favorite lot.*

A. Establish that there is one lot which is better for your customer than all the others.

B. Fear of loss is a tremendous motivator, and is even more powerful when combined with jealousy. Create, therefore, not only the fear of loss, but also the image of someone else benefitting from that loss.

8. *Ask for the order.*

A. If SAM has been executed effectively, then this stage needs to be no more complex than asking "Would you like to have it?"

B. Your close must be compatible with your own personality, and with your demeanor and presentation up to that point.

One of the advantages of SAM is that it works essentially the same in good markets and bad. In slower markets you may choose to ease into the selling process more casually during the first ten minutes, as you set about establishing rapport. In slower times negotiating may play a more significant role at the end, but do everything you can to keep SAM intact between the beginning and the end. Then add the negotiation stage on to the end of SAM, after you fully understand your customer's position and they understand yours.

In overcoming objections, the mentality developed here includes the following elements:
1. An objection is not the same as a rejection. Evaluate the objection as described in Chapter Three and, whenever possible, consider it as a step toward the sale rather than as an obstacle to it.
2. An objection is most often an unfavorable comparison in your customer's mind between what his ideal is and what you are actually offering. You must reorient your customer so that he is comparing what you are offering to his current situation, and to what alternatives really exist in your location and price range.
3. You are selling a total package, not just a list of unrelated components. Your customer's real choices are:
   a. Your total package;
   b. Someone else's total package.
   c. Where the customer is living now.

When your customer attacks individual components of your package, deal with those objections specifically, but always reinforce your package as a whole. Your total package — not the individual components of that package — is where your customers will find your value. The total package is also where your customers will have their most important needs met. This is another reason why concept selling is so critical.

Preparation has been emphasized here as an important part of the mentality because it helps sustain your focus and your momentum, and also helps to increase your credibility with your customer. Preparation includes:
1. Understanding of your business, your market, your location and your competition.
2. Having a technical understanding of the construction and engineering features of your product which may benefit your customer.
3. Keeping a diary.
4. Writing scripts (more for purposes of anticipation than memorization).
5. Having readily available anecdotes and third-party endorse-

ments for as many potential situations as possible.

Unlike selling many less expensive products, selling new homes must be "comfortable" — for the salesperson and for the customer. Selling a home is rarely a victory in a battle of wills. More often it is a matter of increasing the buyer's comfort level to the point where the sale becomes the natural result. A comfortable environment is easier for the salesperson to control.

Product demonstration, showing lots and follow up should be viewed as services. This helps keep the elements of the selling process more comfortable for you, and consequently for your customer.

The following selling dynamics are a natural part of your **Strategy to Achieve Momentum** and are part of your **Successful Sales Mentality:**

1. Establishing rapport.
2. Concept selling.
3. Identifying and fulfilling needs.
4. Emotional selling.
5. Creating urgency.

Focusing on these five dynamics will help you control the selling environment.

Out of this **Successful Sales Mentality** can emerge the behavioral patterns and techniques which more easily direct the selling process toward a close which is a conclusion rather than a crisis.

Selling new homes has a natural rhythm to it. The heartbeat of this rhythm is momentum. The characteristics of success discussed in Chapter One have helped salespeople to use that rhythm to their maximum advantage. This book has incorporated those characteristics into a mentality and strategy which can help you to achieve success more quickly and sustain it throughout your career.

About The Author

Richard Tiller began his career in new home sales in 1972. His extraordinary track record includes single family homes, townhomes and condominiums, and he sold new homes successfully in the housing recessions which began each of the last three decades. He has spent seven years in sales and marketing management, and has served the industry in many volunteer capacities, including speaker, writer, consultant and sales trainer. He has also served on local and national judging committees for sales and marketing. His company, Tiller Marketing Services, is located near Washington, D.C.